T&P BOOKS

ARABIC
VOCABULARY

FOR ENGLISH SPEAKERS

ENGLISH ARABIC

The most useful words
To expand your lexicon and sharpen
your language skills

3000 words

Egyptian Arabic vocabulary for English speakers - 3000 words
By Andrey Taranov

T&P Books vocabularies are intended for helping you learn, memorize and review foreign words. The dictionary is divided into themes, covering all major spheres of everyday activities, business, science, culture, etc.

The process of learning words using T&P Books' theme-based dictionaries gives you the following advantages:

- Correctly grouped source information predetermines success at subsequent stages of word memorization
- Availability of words derived from the same root allowing memorization of word units (rather than separate words)
- Small units of words facilitate the process of establishing associative links needed for consolidation of vocabulary
- Level of language knowledge can be estimated by the number of learned words

T&P Books Publishing
www.tpbooks.com

ISBN: 978-1-78716-706-3

This book is also available in E-book formats.
Please visit www.tpbooks.com or the major online bookstores.

EGYPTIAN ARABIC VOCABULARY
for English speakers

T&P Books vocabularies are intended to help you learn, memorize, and review foreign words. The vocabulary contains over 3000 commonly used words arranged thematically.

- Vocabulary contains the most commonly used words
- Recommended as an addition to any language course
- Meets the needs of beginners and advanced learners of foreign languages
- Convenient for daily use, revision sessions, and self-testing activities
- Allows you to assess your vocabulary

Special features of the vocabulary

- Words are organized according to their meaning, not alphabetically
- Words are presented in three columns to facilitate the reviewing and self-testing processes
- Words in groups are divided into small blocks to facilitate the learning process
- The vocabulary offers a convenient and simple transcription of each foreign word

The vocabulary has 101 topics including:

Basic Concepts, Numbers, Colors, Months, Seasons, Units of Measurement, Clothing & Accessories, Food & Nutrition, Restaurant, Family Members, Relatives, Character, Feelings, Emotions, Diseases, City, Town, Sightseeing, Shopping, Money, House, Home, Office, Working in the Office, Import & Export, Marketing, Job Search, Sports, Education, Computer, Internet, Tools, Nature, Countries, Nationalities and more ...

T&P BOOKS' THEME-BASED DICTIONARIES

The Correct System for Memorizing Foreign Words

Acquiring vocabulary is one of the most important elements of learning a foreign language, because words allow us to express our thoughts, ask questions, and provide answers. An inadequate vocabulary can impede communication with a foreigner and make it difficult to understand a book or movie well.

The pace of activity in all spheres of modern life, including the learning of modern languages, has increased. Today, we need to memorize large amounts of information (grammar rules, foreign words, etc.) within a short period. However, this does not need to be difficult. All you need to do is to choose the right training materials, learn a few special techniques, and develop your individual training system.

Having a system is critical to the process of language learning. Many people fail to succeed in this regard; they cannot master a foreign language because they fail to follow a system comprised of selecting materials, organizing lessons, arranging new words to be learned, and so on. The lack of a system causes confusion and eventually, lowers self-confidence.

T&P Books' theme-based dictionaries can be included in the list of elements needed for creating an effective system for learning foreign words. These dictionaries were specially developed for learning purposes and are meant to help students effectively memorize words and expand their vocabulary.

Generally speaking, the process of learning words consists of three main elements:

- Reception (creation or acquisition) of a training material, such as a word list
- Work aimed at memorizing new words
- Work aimed at reviewing the learned words, such as self-testing

All three elements are equally important since they determine the quality of work and the final result. All three processes require certain skills and a well-thought-out approach.

New words are often encountered quite randomly when learning a foreign language and it may be difficult to include them all in a unified list. As a result, these words remain written on scraps of paper, in book margins, textbooks, and so on. In order to systematize such words, we have to create and continually update a "book of new words." A paper notebook, a netbook, or a tablet PC can be used for these purposes.

This "book of new words" will be your personal, unique list of words. However, it will only contain the words that you came across during the learning process. For example, you might have written down the words "Sunday," "Tuesday," and "Friday." However, there are additional words for days of the week, for example, "Saturday," that are missing, and your list of words would be incomplete. Using a theme dictionary, in addition to the "book of new words," is a reasonable solution to this problem.

The theme-based dictionary may serve as the basis for expanding your vocabulary.

It will be your big "book of new words" containing the most frequently used words of a foreign language already included. There are quite a few theme-based dictionaries available, and you should ensure that you make the right choice in order to get the maximum benefit from your purchase.

Therefore, we suggest using theme-based dictionaries from T&P Books Publishing as an aid to learning foreign words. Our books are specially developed for effective use in the sphere of vocabulary systematization, expansion and review.

Theme-based dictionaries are not a magical solution to learning new words. However, they can serve as your main database to aid foreign-language acquisition. Apart from theme dictionaries, you can have copybooks for writing down new words, flash cards, glossaries for various texts, as well as other resources; however, a good theme dictionary will always remain your primary collection of words.

T&P Books' theme-based dictionaries are specialty books that contain the most frequently used words in a language.

The main characteristic of such dictionaries is the division of words into themes. For example, the *City* theme contains the words "street," "crossroads," "square," "fountain," and so on. The *Talking* theme might contain words like "to talk," "to ask," "question," and "answer".

All the words in a theme are divided into smaller units, each comprising 3–5 words. Such an arrangement improves the perception of words and makes the learning process less tiresome. Each unit contains a selection of words with similar meanings or identical roots. This allows you to learn words in small groups and establish other associative links that have a positive effect on memorization.

The words on each page are placed in three columns: a word in your native language, its translation, and its transcription. Such positioning allows for the use of techniques for effective memorization. After closing the translation column, you can flip through and review foreign words, and vice versa. "This is an easy and convenient method of review – one that we recommend you do often."

Our theme-based dictionaries contain transcriptions for all the foreign words. Unfortunately, none of the existing transcriptions are able to convey the exact nuances of foreign pronunciation. That is why we recommend using the transcriptions only as a supplementary learning aid. Correct pronunciation can only be acquired with the help of sound. Therefore our collection includes audio theme-based dictionaries.

The process of learning words using T&P Books' theme-based dictionaries gives you the following advantages:

- You have correctly grouped source information, which predetermines your success at subsequent stages of word memorization
- Availability of words derived from the same root (lazy, lazily, lazybones), allowing you to memorize word units instead of separate words
- Small units of words facilitate the process of establishing associative links needed for consolidation of vocabulary
- You can estimate the number of learned words and hence your level of language knowledge
- The dictionary allows for the creation of an effective and high-quality revision process
- You can revise certain themes several times, modifying the revision methods and techniques
- Audio versions of the dictionaries help you to work out the pronunciation of words and develop your skills of auditory word perception

The T&P Books' theme-based dictionaries are offered in several variants differing in the number of words: 1.500, 3.000, 5.000, 7.000, and 9.000 words. There are also dictionaries containing 15,000 words for some language combinations. Your choice of dictionary will depend on your knowledge level and goals.

We sincerely believe that our dictionaries will become your trusty assistant in learning foreign languages and will allow you to easily acquire the necessary vocabulary.

TABLE OF CONTENTS

FAUNA

FLORA

COUNTRIES OF THE WORLD

PRONUNCIATION GUIDE

T&P phonetic alphabet	Egyptian Arabic example	English example
[a]	[ṭaffa] طفّى	shorter than in ask
[ā]	[eχtār] إختار	calf, palm
[e]	[setta] ستّة	elm, medal
[i]	[minā'] ميناء	shorter than in feet
[ī]	[ebrīl] إبريل	feet, meter
[o]	[oɣosṭos] أغسطس	pod, John
[ō]	[ḥalazōn] حلزون	fall, bomb
[u]	[kalkutta] كلكتا	book
[ū]	[gamūs] جاموس	fuel, tuna
[b]	[bedāya] بداية	baby, book
[d]	[sa'āda] سعادة	day, doctor
[ḍ]	[waḍ'] وضع	[d] pharyngeal
[ʒ]	[arʒantīn] الأرجنتين	forge, pleasure
[ẓ]	[ẓahar] ظهر	[z] pharyngeal
[f]	[χafīf] خفيف	face, food
[g]	[bahga] بهجة	game, gold
[h]	[ettegāh] إتّجاه	home, have
[ḥ]	[ḥabb] حبّ	[h] pharyngeal
[y]	[dahaby] ذهبي	yes, New York
[k]	[korsy] كرسي	clock, kiss
[l]	[lammaḥ] لمّح	lace, people
[m]	[marṣad] مرصد	magic, milk
[n]	[ganūb] جنوب	sang, thing
[p]	[kaputʃino] كابتشينو	pencil, private
[q]	[wasaq] وثق	king, club
[r]	[roḥe] روح	rice, radio
[s]	[soχreya] سخرية	city, boss
[ṣ]	[me'ṣam] معصم	[s] pharyngeal
[ʃ]	['aʃā'] عشاء	machine, shark
[t]	[tanūb] تنوب	tourist, trip
[ṭ]	[χarīṭa] خريطة	[t] pharyngeal
[θ]	[mamūθ] ماموث	month, tooth
[v]	[vietnām] فيتنام	very, river
[w]	[wadda'] ودّع	vase, winter
[χ]	[baχīl] بخيل	as in Scots 'loch'
[ɣ]	[etɣadda] إتغدّى	between [g] and [h]

T&P phonetic alphabet	Egyptian Arabic example	English example
[z]	[me'za] معزة	zebra, please
['] (ayn)	[sab'a] سبعة	voiced pharyngeal fricative
['] (hamza)	[sa'al] سأل	glottal stop

ABBREVIATIONS used in the vocabulary

Egyptian Arabic abbreviations

du	-	plural noun (double)
f	-	feminine noun
m	-	masculine noun
pl	-	plural

English abbreviations

ab.	-	about
adj	-	adjective
adv	-	adverb
anim.	-	animate
as adj	-	attributive noun used as adjective
e.g.	-	for example
etc.	-	et cetera
fam.	-	familiar
fem.	-	feminine
form.	-	formal
inanim.	-	inanimate
masc.	-	masculine
math	-	mathematics
mil.	-	military
n	-	noun
pl	-	plural
pron.	-	pronoun
sb	-	somebody
sing.	-	singular
sth	-	something
v aux	-	auxiliary verb
vi	-	intransitive verb
vi, vt	-	intransitive, transitive verb
vt	-	transitive verb

BASIC CONCEPTS

1. Pronouns

I, me	ana	أنا
you (masc.)	enta	أنت
you (fem.)	enty	أنت
he	howwa	هوّ
she	hiya	هيّ
we	eḥna	إحنا
you (to a group)	antom	أنتم
they	hamm	همّ

2. Greetings. Salutations

Hello! (form.)	assalamu ʻalaykum!	السلام عليكم!
Good morning!	ṣabāḥ el χeyr!	صباح الخير!
Good afternoon!	neharak saʻīd!	نهارك سعيد!
Good evening!	masāʾ el χeyr!	مساء الخير!
to say hello	sallem	سلّم
Hi! (hello)	ahlan!	أهلاً!
greeting (n)	salām (m)	سلام
to greet (vt)	sallem ʻala	سلّم على
How are you?	ezzayek?	ازّيّك؟
What's new?	aχbārak eyh?	أخبارك ايه؟
Bye-Bye! Goodbye!	maʻ el salāma!	مع السلامة!
See you soon!	aʃūfak orayeb!	أشوفك قريب!
Farewell!	maʻ el salāma!	مع السلامة!
to say goodbye	waddaʻ	ودّع
So long!	bay bay!	باي باي!
Thank you!	ʃokran!	شكراً!
Thank you very much!	ʃokran geddan!	شكراً جداً!
You're welcome	el ʻafw	العفو
Don't mention it!	la ʃokr ʻala wāgeb	لا شكر على واجب
It was nothing	el ʻafw	العفو
Excuse me! (fam.)	ʻan eznak!	عن إذنك!
Excuse me! (form.)	baʻd ezn ḥadretak!	بعد إذن حضرتك!
to excuse (forgive)	ʻazar	عذر

to apologize (vi)	e'tazar	أعتذر
My apologies	ana 'āsef	أنا آسف
I'm sorry!	ana 'āsef!	أنا آسف!
to forgive (vt)	'afa	عفا
please (adv)	men faḍlak	من فضلك
Don't forget!	ma tensāʃ!	ما تنساش!
Certainly!	ṭab'an!	طبعاً!
Of course not!	la' ṭab'an!	لأ طبعاً!
Okay! (I agree)	ettafa'na!	إتّفقنا!
That's enough!	kefāya!	كفاية!

3. Questions

Who?	mīn?	مين؟
What?	eyh?	ايه؟
Where? (at, in)	feyn?	فين؟
Where (to)?	feyn?	فين؟
From where?	meneyn?	منين؟
When?	emta	امتى؟
Why? (What for?)	'aʃān eyh?	عشان ايه؟
Why? (~ are you crying?)	leyh?	ليه؟
What for?	l eyh?	لـ ليه؟
How? (in what way)	ezāy?	إزاي؟
What? (What kind of ...?)	eyh?	ايه؟
Which?	ayī?	أيّ؟
To whom?	le mīn?	لمين؟
About whom?	'an mīn?	عن مين؟
About what?	'an eyh?	عن ايه؟
With whom?	ma' mīn?	مع مين؟
How many? How much?	kām?	كام؟
Whose?	betā'et mīn?	بتاعت مين؟

4. Prepositions

with (accompanied by)	ma'	مع
without	men ɣeyr	من غير
to (indicating direction)	ela	إلى
about (talking ~ ...)	'an	عن
before (in time)	'abl	قبل
in front of ...	'oddām	قدّام
under (beneath, below)	taḥt	تحت
above (over)	fo'e	فوق
on (atop)	'ala	على

from (off, out of)	men	من
of (made from)	men	من
in (e.g., ~ ten minutes)	ba'd	بعد
over (across the top of)	men 'ala	من على

5. Function words. Adverbs. Part 1

Where? (at, in)	feyn?	فين؟
here (adv)	hena	هنا
there (adv)	henāk	هناك
somewhere (to be)	fe makānen ma	في مكان ما
nowhere (not anywhere)	meʃ fi ayī makān	مش في أيّ مكان
by (near, beside)	ganb	جنب
by the window	ganb el ʃebbāk	جنب الشبّاك
Where (to)?	feyn?	فين؟
here (e.g., come ~!)	hena	هنا
there (e.g., to go ~)	henāk	هناك
from here (adv)	men hena	من هنا
from there (adv)	men henāk	من هناك
close (adv)	'arīb	قريب
far (adv)	be'īd	بعيد
near (e.g., ~ Paris)	'and	عند
nearby (adv)	'arīb	قريب
not far (adv)	meʃ be'īd	مش بعيد
left (adj)	el ʃemāl	الشمال
on the left	'alal ʃemāl	على الشمال
to the left	lel ʃemāl	للشمال
right (adj)	el yemīn	اليمين
on the right	'alal yemīn	على اليمين
to the right	lel yemīn	لليمين
in front (adv)	'oddām	قدّام
front (as adj)	amāmy	أمامي
ahead (the kids ran ~)	ela el amām	إلى الأمام
behind (adv)	wara'	وراء
from behind	men wara	من ورا
back (towards the rear)	le wara	لورا
middle	wasaṭ (m)	وسط
in the middle	fel wasat	في الوسط
at the side	'ala ganb	على جنب

everywhere (adv)	fe kol makān	في كل مكان
around (in all directions)	ḥawaleyn	حوالين
from inside	men gowwah	من جوّه
somewhere (to go)	le ʼayī makān	لأي مكان
straight (directly)	ʻala ṭūl	على طول
back (e.g., come ~)	rogūʻ	رجوع
from anywhere	men ayī makān	من أيّ مكان
from somewhere	men makānen mā	من مكان ما
firstly (adv)	awwalan	أوّلاً
secondly (adv)	sāneyan	ثانياً
thirdly (adv)	sālesan	ثالثاً
suddenly (adv)	fagʼa	فجأة
at first (in the beginning)	fel bedāya	في البداية
for the first time	le ʼawwel marra	لأوّل مرّة
long before ...	ʼabl ... be modda ṭawīla	قبل... بمدة طويلة
anew (over again)	men gedīd	من جديد
for good (adv)	lel abad	للأبد
never (adv)	abadan	أبداً
again (adv)	tāny	تاني
now (adv)	delwaʼty	دلوقتي
often (adv)	ketīr	كثير
then (adv)	waʼtaha	وقتها
urgently (quickly)	ʻala ṭūl	على طول
usually (adv)	ʻādatan	عادةً
by the way, ...	ʻala fekra ...	على فكرة...
possible (that is ~)	momken	ممكن
probably (adv)	momken	ممكن
maybe (adv)	momken	ممكن
besides ...	bel eḍāfa ela ...	بالإضافة إلى...
that's why ...	ʻaʃān keda	عشان كده
in spite of ...	bel raɣm men ...	بالرغم من...
thanks to ...	be faḍl ...	بفضل...
what (pron.)	elly	إللي
that (conj.)	ennu	إنّه
something	ḥāga (f)	حاجة
anything (something)	ayī ḥāga (f)	أيّ حاجة
nothing	wala ḥāga	ولا حاجة
who (pron.)	elly	إللي
someone	ḥadd	حدّ
somebody	ḥadd	حدّ
nobody	wala ḥadd	ولا حدّ
nowhere (a voyage to ~)	meʃ le wala makān	مش لـ ولا مكان
nobody's	wala ḥadd	ولا حدّ

somebody's	le ḥadd	لحدّ
so (I'm ~ glad)	geddan	جداً
also (as well)	kamān	كمان
too (as well)	kamān	كمان

6. Function words. Adverbs. Part 2

Why?	leyh?	ليه؟
for some reason	le sabeben ma	لسبب ما
because ...	ʿaʃān ...	... عشان
for some purpose	le hadafen mā	لهدف ما
and	w	و
or	walla	ولّا
but	bass	بسّ
for (e.g., ~ me)	ʿaʃān	عشان
too (~ many people)	ketīr geddan	كتير جدّاً
only (exclusively)	bass	بسّ
exactly (adv)	bel ḍabṭ	بالضبط
about (more or less)	naḥw	نحو
approximately (adv)	naḥw	نحو
approximate (adj)	taqrīby	تقريبي
almost (adv)	ta'rīban	تقريباً
the rest	el bā'y (m)	الباقي
each (adj)	koll	كلّ
any (no matter which)	ayī	أيّ
many, much (a lot of)	ketīr	كتير
many people	nās ketīr	ناس كتير
all (everyone)	koll el nās	كلّ الناس
in return for ...	fi moqābel ...	... في مقابل
in exchange (adv)	fe moqābel	في مقابل
by hand (made)	bel yad	باليد
hardly (negative opinion)	bel kād	بالكاد
probably (adv)	momken	ممكن
on purpose (intentionally)	bel 'aṣd	بالقصد
by accident (adv)	bel ṣodfa	بالصدفة
very (adv)	'awy	قويّ
for example (adv)	masalan	مثلاً
between	beyn	بين
among	wesṭ	وسط
so much (such a lot)	ketīr	كتير
especially (adv)	χāṣṣa	خاصّة

NUMBERS. MISCELLANEOUS

7. Cardinal numbers. Part 1

0 zero	ṣefr	صفر
1 one	wāḥed	واحد
1 one (fem.)	waḥda	واحدة
2 two	etneyn	إتنين
3 three	talāta	ثلاثة
4 four	arba'a	أربعة
5 five	χamsa	خمسة
6 six	setta	ستّة
7 seven	sab'a	سبعة
8 eight	tamanya	ثمانية
9 nine	tes'a	تسعة
10 ten	'aʃara	عشرة
11 eleven	ḥedāʃar	حداشر
12 twelve	etnāʃar	إتناشر
13 thirteen	talattāʃar	تلاتّاشر
14 fourteen	arba'tāʃer	أربعتاشر
15 fifteen	χamastāʃer	خمستاشر
16 sixteen	settāʃar	ستّاشر
17 seventeen	saba'tāʃar	سبعتاشر
18 eighteen	tamantāʃar	تمنتاشر
19 nineteen	tes'atāʃar	تسعتاشر
20 twenty	'eʃrīn	عشرين
21 twenty-one	wāḥed we 'eʃrīn	واحد وعشرين
22 twenty-two	etneyn we 'eʃrīn	إتنين وعشرين
23 twenty-three	talāta we 'eʃrīn	ثلاثة وعشرين
30 thirty	talatīn	ثلاثين
31 thirty-one	wāḥed we talatīn	واحد وتلاتين
32 thirty-two	etneyn we talatīn	إتنين وتلاتين
33 thirty-three	talāta we talatīn	ثلاثة وثلاثين
40 forty	arbe'īn	أربعين
41 forty-one	wāḥed we arbe'īn	واحد وأربعين
42 forty-two	etneyn we arbe'īn	إتنين وأربعين
43 forty-three	talāta we arbe'īn	ثلاثة وأربعين
50 fifty	χamsīn	خمسين
51 fifty-one	wāḥed we χamsīn	واحد وخمسين

52 fifty-two	etneyn we χamsīn	إتنين وخمسين
53 fifty-three	talāta we χamsīn	ثلاثة وخمسين
60 sixty	settīn	ستّين
61 sixty-one	wāḥed we settīn	واحد وستّين
62 sixty-two	etneyn we settīn	إتنين وستّين
63 sixty-three	talāta we settīn	ثلاثة وستّين
70 seventy	sabʿīn	سبعين
71 seventy-one	wāḥed we sabʿīn	واحد وسبعين
72 seventy-two	etneyn we sabʿīn	إتنين وسبعين
73 seventy-three	talāta we sabʿīn	ثلاثة وسبعين
80 eighty	tamanīn	ثمانين
81 eighty-one	wāḥed we tamanīn	واحد وتمانين
82 eighty-two	etneyn we tamanīn	إتنين وتمانين
83 eighty-three	talāta we tamanīn	ثلاثة وثمانين
90 ninety	tesʿīn	تسعين
91 ninety-one	wāḥed we tesʿīn	واحد وتسعين
92 ninety-two	etneyn we tesʿīn	إتنين وتسعين
93 ninety-three	talāta we tesʿīn	ثلاثة وتسعين

8. Cardinal numbers. Part 2

100 one hundred	miya	ميّة
200 two hundred	meteyn	ميتين
300 three hundred	toltomiya	تلتميّة
400 four hundred	robʿomiya	ربعميّة
500 five hundred	χomsomiya	خمسميّة
600 six hundred	sotomiya	ستميّة
700 seven hundred	sobʿomiya	سبعميّة
800 eight hundred	tomnome'a	ثمنمئة
900 nine hundred	tosʿomiya	تسعميّة
1000 one thousand	alf	ألف
2000 two thousand	alfeyn	ألفين
3000 three thousand	talat 'ālāf	ثلاث آلاف
10000 ten thousand	ʿaʃaret 'ālāf	عشرة آلاف
one hundred thousand	mīt alf	ميت ألف
million	millyon (m)	مليون
billion	millyār (m)	مليار

9. Ordinal numbers

first (adj)	awwel	أوّل
second (adj)	tāny	ثاني

third (adj)	tālet	ثالث
fourth (adj)	rābeʿ	رابع
fifth (adj)	χāmes	خامس
sixth (adj)	sādes	سادس
seventh (adj)	sābeʿ	سابع
eighth (adj)	tāmen	ثامن
ninth (adj)	tāseʿ	تاسع
tenth (adj)	ʿāʃer	عاشر

COLOURS. UNITS OF MEASUREMENT

10. Colors

color	lone (m)	لون
shade (tint)	daraget el lōn (m)	درجة اللون
hue	ṣabɣet lōn (f)	صبغة اللون
rainbow	qose qozaḥ (m)	قوس قزح
white (adj)	abyaḍ	أبيض
black (adj)	aswad	أسود
gray (adj)	romādy	رمادي
green (adj)	aχḍar	أخضر
yellow (adj)	aṣfar	أصفر
red (adj)	aḥmar	أحمر
blue (adj)	azra'	أزرق
light blue (adj)	azra' fāteḥ	أزرق فاتح
pink (adj)	wardy	وردي
orange (adj)	bortoqāly	برتقاليّ
violet (adj)	banaffsegy	بنفّسجي
brown (adj)	bonny	بنّي
golden (adj)	dahaby	ذهبي
silvery (adj)	feḍḍy	فضّي
beige (adj)	bɛ:ʒ	بيج
cream (adj)	ʿāgy	عاجيّ
turquoise (adj)	fayrūzy	فيروزي
cherry red (adj)	aḥmar karazy	أحمر كرزي
lilac (adj)	laylaky	ليّلكي
crimson (adj)	qormozy	قرمزي
light (adj)	fāteḥ	فاتح
dark (adj)	ɣāme'	غامق
bright, vivid (adj)	zāhy	زاهي
colored (pencils)	melawwen	ملوّن
color (e.g., ~ film)	melawwen	ملوّن
black-and-white (adj)	abyaḍ we aswad	أبيض وأسوّد
plain (one-colored)	sāda	سادة
multicolored (adj)	motaʿadded el alwān	متعددّ الألوان

11. Units of measurement

weight	wazn (m)	وزن
length	ṭūl (m)	طول
width	ʿarḍ (m)	عرض
height	ertefāʿ (m)	إرتفاع
depth	ʿomq (m)	عمق
volume	ḥagm (m)	حجم
area	mesāḥa (f)	مساحة
gram	gram (m)	جرام
milligram	milligrām (m)	ملّيغرام
kilogram	kilogrām (m)	كيلوغرام
ton	ṭenn (m)	طنّ
pound	reṭl (m)	رطل
ounce	onṣa (f)	أونصة
meter	metr (m)	متر
millimeter	millimetr (m)	ملّيمتر
centimeter	santimetr (m)	سنتيمتر
kilometer	kilometr (m)	كيلومتر
mile	mīl (m)	ميل
inch	boṣa (f)	بوصة
foot	ʾadam (m)	قدم
yard	yarda (f)	ياردة
square meter	metr morabbaʿ (m)	متر مربّع
hectare	hektār (m)	هكتار
liter	litre (m)	لتر
degree	daraga (f)	درجة
volt	volt (m)	فولت
ampere	ambere (m)	أمبير
horsepower	ḥoṣān (m)	حصان
quantity	kemiya (f)	كميّة
a little bit of ...	ʃewayet ...	شويّة...
half	noṣṣ (m)	نصّ
dozen	desta (f)	دستة
piece (item)	waḥda (f)	وحدة
size	ḥagm (m)	حجم
scale (map ~)	meʾyās (m)	مقياس
minimal (adj)	el adna	الأدنى
the smallest (adj)	el aṣɣar	الأصغر
medium (adj)	motawasseṭ	متوّسط
maximal (adj)	el aqṣa	الأقصى
the largest (adj)	el akbar	الأكبر

12. Containers

canning jar (glass ~)	barṭamān (m)	برطمان
can	kanz (m)	كانز
bucket	gardal (m)	جردل
barrel	barmīl (m)	برميل
wash basin (e.g., plastic ~)	ḥoḍe lel ɣasīl (m)	حوض للغسيل
tank (100L water ~)	χazzān (m)	خزّان
hip flask	zamzamiya (f)	زمزميّة
jerrycan	ʒerken (m)	جركن
tank (e.g., tank car)	χazzān (m)	خزّان
mug	mugg (m)	ماجّ
cup (of coffee, etc.)	fengān (m)	فنجان
saucer	ṭaba' fengān (m)	طبق فنجان
glass (tumbler)	kobbāya (f)	كوبّاية
wine glass	kāsa (f)	كاسة
stock pot (soup pot)	ḥalla (f)	حلّة
bottle (~ of wine)	ezāza (f)	إزازة
neck (of the bottle, etc.)	'onq (m)	عنق
carafe (decanter)	dawra' zogāgy (m)	دورّق زجاجي
pitcher	ebrī' (m)	إبريق
vessel (container)	we'ā' (m)	وعاء
pot (crock, stoneware ~)	aṣīṣ (m)	أصيص
vase	vāza (f)	فازة
bottle (perfume ~)	ezāza (f)	إزازة
vial, small bottle	ezāza (f)	إزازة
tube (of toothpaste)	anbūba (f)	أنبوبة
sack (bag)	kīs (m)	كيس
bag (paper ~, plastic ~)	kīs (m)	كيس
pack (of cigarettes, etc.)	'elba (f)	علبة
box (e.g., shoebox)	'elba (f)	علبة
crate	ṣandū' (m)	صندوق
basket	salla (f)	سلّة

MAIN VERBS

13. The most important verbs. Part 1

to advise (vt)	naṣaḥ	نصح
to agree (say yes)	ettafa'	إتّفق
to answer (vi, vt)	gāwab	جاوب
to apologize (vi)	e'tazar	إعتذر
to arrive (vi)	weṣel	وصل
to ask (~ oneself)	sa'al	سأل
to ask (~ sb to do sth)	ṭalab	طلب
to be (vi)	kān	كان
to be afraid	χāf	خاف
to be hungry	'āyez 'ākol	عايز آكل
to be interested in ...	ehtamm be	إهتمّ بـ
to be needed	maṭlūb	مطلوب
to be surprised	etfāge'	إتفاجئ
to be thirsty	'āyez aʃrab	عايز أشرب
to begin (vt)	bada'	بدأ
to belong to ...	χaṣṣ	خصّ
to boast (vi)	tabāha	تباهى
to break (split into pieces)	kasar	كسر
to call (~ for help)	estaɣās	إستغاث
can (v aux)	'eder	قدر
to catch (vt)	mesek	مسك
to change (vt)	ɣayar	غيّر
to choose (select)	eχtār	إختار
to come down (the stairs)	nezel	نزل
to compare (vt)	qāran	قارن
to complain (vi, vt)	ʃaka	شكا
to confuse (mix up)	etlaχbaṭ	إتلخبط
to continue (vt)	wāṣel	واصل
to control (vt)	et-ḥakkem	إتحكّم
to cook (dinner)	ḥaḍḍar	حضّر
to cost (vt)	kallef	كلّف
to count (add up)	'add	عدّ
to count on ...	e'tamad 'ala ...	إعتمد على...
to create (vt)	'amal	عمل
to cry (weep)	baka	بكى

14. The most important verbs. Part 2

to deceive (vi, vt)	xada'	خدع
to decorate (tree, street)	zayen	زيّن
to defend (a country, etc.)	dāfa'	دافع
to demand (request firmly)	ṭāleb	طالب
to dig (vt)	ḥafar	حفر
to discuss (vt)	nā'eʃ	ناقش
to do (vt)	'amal	عمل
to doubt (have doubts)	ʃakk fe	شكّ في
to drop (let fall)	wa''a'	وقّع
to enter (room, house, etc.)	daxal	دخل
to exist (vi)	kān mawgūd	كان موّجود
to expect (foresee)	tanabba'	تنبّأ
to explain (vt)	ʃaraḥ	شرح
to fall (vi)	we'e'	وقع
to find (vt)	la'a	لقى
to finish (vt)	xallaṣ	خلّص
to fly (vi)	ṭār	طار
to follow ... (come after)	tatabba'	تتبّع
to forget (vi, vt)	nesy	نسي
to forgive (vt)	'afa	عفا
to give (vt)	edda	إدّى
to give a hint	edda lamḥa	إدّى لمحة
to go (on foot)	meʃy	مشى
to go for a swim	sebeḥ	سبح
to go out (for dinner, etc.)	xarag	خرج
to guess (the answer)	xammen	خمّن
to have (vt)	malak	ملك
to have breakfast	feṭer	فطر
to have dinner	et'asʃa	إتعشّى
to have lunch	etɣadda	إتغدّى
to hear (vt)	seme'	سمع
to help (vt)	sā'ed	ساعد
to hide (vt)	xabba	خبّأ
to hope (vi, vt)	tamanna	تمنّى
to hunt (vi, vt)	eṣṭād	اصطاد
to hurry (vi)	esta'gel	إستعجل

15. The most important verbs. Part 3

to inform (vt)	'āl ly	قال لي
to insist (vi, vt)	aṣarr	أصرّ

to insult (vt)	ahān	أهان
to invite (vt)	ʿazam	عزم
to joke (vi)	hazzar	هزّر
to keep (vt)	ḥafaẓ	حفظ
to keep silent	seket	سكت
to kill (vt)	ʾatal	قتل
to know (sb)	ʿeref	عرف
to know (sth)	ʿeref	عرف
to laugh (vi)	ḍeḥek	ضحك
to liberate (city, etc.)	ḥarrar	حرّر
to like (I like ...)	ʿagab	عجب
to look for ... (search)	dawwar ʿala	دوّر على
to love (sb)	ḥabb	حبّ
to make a mistake	ɣeleṭ	غلط
to manage, to run	adār	أدار
to mean (signify)	ʾaṣad	قصد
to mention (talk about)	zakar	ذكر
to miss (school, etc.)	ɣāb	غاب
to notice (see)	lāḥaẓ	لاحظ
to object (vi, vt)	eʿtaraḍ	إعترض
to observe (see)	rāqab	راقب
to open (vt)	fataḥ	فتح
to order (meal, etc.)	ṭalab	طلب
to order (mil.)	amar	أمر
to own (possess)	malak	ملك
to participate (vi)	ʃārek	شارك
to pay (vi, vt)	dafaʿ	دفع
to permit (vt)	samaḥ	سمح
to plan (vt)	χaṭṭeṭ	خطّط
to play (children)	leʿeb	لعب
to pray (vi, vt)	ṣalla	صلّى
to prefer (vt)	faḍḍal	فضّل
to promise (vt)	waʿad	وعد
to pronounce (vt)	naṭaʾ	نطق
to propose (vt)	ʿaraḍ	عرض
to punish (vt)	ʿāqab	عاقب

16. The most important verbs. Part 4

to read (vi, vt)	ʾara	قرأ
to recommend (vt)	naṣaḥ	نصح
to refuse (vi, vt)	rafaḍ	رفض
to regret (be sorry)	nedem	ندم
to rent (sth from sb)	estʾgar	إستأجر

to repeat (say again)	karrar	كرّر
to reserve, to book	ḥagaz	حجز
to run (vi)	gery	جري
to save (rescue)	anqaz	أنقذ
to say (~ thank you)	'āl	قال
to scold (vt)	wabbeχ	وبّخ
to see (vt)	ʃāf	شاف
to sell (vt)	bāʿ	باع
to send (vt)	arsal	أرسل
to shoot (vi)	ḍarab bel nār	ضرب بالنار
to shout (vi)	ṣarraχ	صرّخ
to show (vt)	warra	ورّى
to sign (document)	waqqaʿ	وقّع
to sit down (vi)	'aʿad	قعد
to smile (vi)	ebtasam	إبتسم
to speak (vi, vt)	kallem	كلّم
to steal (money, etc.)	sara'	سرق
to stop (for pause, etc.)	wa''af	وقّف
to stop (please ~ calling me)	baṭṭal	بطّل
to study (vt)	daras	درس
to swim (vi)	ʿām	عام
to take (vt)	aχad	أخد
to think (vi, vt)	fakkar	فكّر
to threaten (vt)	hadded	هدّد
to touch (with hands)	lamas	لمس
to translate (vt)	targem	ترجم
to trust (vt)	wasaq	وثق
to try (attempt)	ḥāwel	حاول
to turn (e.g., ~ left)	ḥād	حاد
to underestimate (vt)	estaχaff	إستخفّ
to understand (vt)	fehem	فهم
to unite (vt)	waḥḥed	وحّد
to wait (vt)	estanna	إستنّى
to want (wish, desire)	ʿāyez	عايز
to warn (vt)	ḥazzar	حذّر
to work (vi)	eʃtaɣal	إشتغل
to write (vt)	katab	كتب
to write down	katab	كتب

TIME. CALENDAR

17. Weekdays

Monday	el etneyn (m)	الإتنين
Tuesday	el talāt (m)	التلات
Wednesday	el arbe'ā' (m)	الأربعاء
Thursday	el χamīs (m)	الخميس
Friday	el gom'a (m)	الجمعة
Saturday	el sabt (m)	السبت
Sunday	el aḥad (m)	الأحد
today (adv)	el naharda	النهارده
tomorrow (adv)	bokra	بكرة
the day after tomorrow	ba'd bokra (m)	بعد بكرة
yesterday (adv)	embāreḥ	امبارح
the day before yesterday	awwel embāreḥ	أوّل امبارح
day	yome (m)	يوم
working day	yome 'amal (m)	يوم عمل
public holiday	agāza rasmiya (f)	أجازة رسميّة
day off	yome el agāza (m)	يوم أجازة
weekend	nehāyet el osbū' (f)	نهاية الأسبوع
all day long	ṭūl el yome	طول اليوم
the next day (adv)	fel yome elly ba'dīh	في اليوم اللي بعديه
two days ago	men yomeyn	من يومين
the day before	fel yome elly 'ablo	في اليوم اللي قبله
daily (adj)	yawmy	يومي
every day (adv)	yawmiyan	يومياً
week	osbū' (m)	أسبوع
last week (adv)	el esbū' elly fāt	الأسبوع اللي فات
next week (adv)	el esbū' elly gayī	الأسبوع اللي جاي
weekly (adj)	osbū'y	أسبوعي
every week (adv)	osbū'iyan	أسبوعياً
twice a week	marreteyn fel osbū'	مرّتين في الأسبوع
every Tuesday	koll solasā'	كلّ ثلاثاء

18. Hours. Day and night

morning	ṣobḥ (m)	صبح
in the morning	fel ṣobḥ	في الصبح
noon, midday	ẓohr (m)	ظهر

in the afternoon	ba'd el ḍohr	بعد الظهر
evening	leyl (m)	ليل
in the evening	bel leyl	بالليل
night	leyl (m)	ليل
at night	bel leyl	بالليل
midnight	noṣṣ el leyl (m)	نصّ الليل
second	sanya (f)	ثانية
minute	deʾīʾa (f)	دقيقة
hour	sā'a (f)	ساعة
half an hour	noṣṣ sā'a (m)	نصّ ساعة
a quarter-hour	rob' sā'a (f)	ربع ساعة
fifteen minutes	χamastāʃer deʾīʾa	خمستاشر دقيقة
24 hours	arba'a we 'eʃrīn sā'a	أربعة وعشرين ساعة
sunrise	ʃorūʾ el ʃams (m)	شروق الشمس
dawn	fagr (m)	فجر
early morning	ṣobḥ badry (m)	صبح بدري
sunset	ɣorūb el ʃams (m)	غروب الشمس
early in the morning	el ṣobḥ badry	الصبح بدري
this morning	el naharda el ṣobḥ	النهاردة الصبح
tomorrow morning	bokra el ṣobḥ	بكرة الصبح
this afternoon	el naharda ba'd el ḍohr	النهاردة بعد الظهر
in the afternoon	ba'd el ḍohr	بعد الظهر
tomorrow afternoon	bokra ba'd el ḍohr	بكرة بعد الظهر
tonight (this evening)	el naharda bel leyl	النهاردة بالليل
tomorrow night	bokra bel leyl	بكرة بالليل
at 3 o'clock sharp	es sā'a talāta bel ḍabṭ	الساعة تلاتة بالضبط
about 4 o'clock	es sā'a arba'a taʾrīban	الساعة أربعة تقريبا
by 12 o'clock	ḥatt es sā'a etnāʃar	حتى الساعة إتناشر
in 20 minutes	fe χelāl 'eʃrīn de'ee'a	في خلال عشرين دقيقة
in an hour	fe χelāl sā'a	في خلال ساعة
on time (adv)	fe maw'edo	في موعده
a quarter of ...	ella rob'	إلّا ربع
within an hour	χelāl sā'a	خلال ساعة
every 15 minutes	koll rob' sā'a	كلّ ربع ساعة
round the clock	leyl nahār	ليل نهار

19. Months. Seasons

January	yanāyer (m)	يناير
February	febrāyer (m)	فبراير
March	māres (m)	مارس
April	ebrīl (m)	إبريل
May	māyo (m)	مايو

June	yonyo (m)	يونيو
July	yolyo (m)	يوليو
August	oɣosṭos (m)	أغسطس
September	sebtamber (m)	سبتمبر
October	oktober (m)	أكتوبر
November	november (m)	نوفمبر
December	desember (m)	ديسمبر
spring	rabeeʿ (m)	ربيع
in spring	fel rabeeʿ	في الربيع
spring (as adj)	rabeeʿy	ربيعي
summer	ṣeyf (m)	صيف
in summer	fel ṣeyf	في الصيف
summer (as adj)	ṣeyfy	صيفي
fall	χarīf (m)	خريف
in fall	fel χarīf	في الخريف
fall (as adj)	χarīfy	خريفي
winter	ʃetāʾ (m)	شتاء
in winter	fel ʃetāʾ	في الشتاء
winter (as adj)	ʃetwy	شتوّي
month	ʃahr (m)	شهر
this month	fel ʃahr da	في الشهر ده
next month	el ʃahr el gayī	الشهر الجايّ
last month	el ʃahr elly fāt	الشهر اللي فات
a month ago	men ʃahr	من شهر
in a month (a month later)	baʿd ʃahr	بعد شهر
in 2 months (2 months later)	baʿd ʃahreyn	بعد شهرين
the whole month	el ʃahr kollo	الشهر كلّه
all month long	ṭawāl el ʃahr	طوال الشهر
monthly (~ magazine)	ʃahry	شهري
monthly (adv)	ʃahry	شهري
every month	koll ʃahr	كلّ شهر
twice a month	marreteyn fel ʃahr	مرّتين في الشهر
year	sana (f)	سنة
this year	el sana di	السنة دي
next year	el sana el gaya	السنة الجايّة
last year	el sana elly fātet	السنة اللي فاتت
a year ago	men sana	من سنة
in a year	baʿd sana	بعد سنة
in two years	baʿd sanateyn	بعد سنتين
the whole year	el sana kollaha	السنة كلّها
all year long	ṭūl el sana	طول السنة
every year	koll sana	كلّ سنة

annual (adj)	sanawy	سنوّي
annually (adv)	koll sana	كلّ سنة
4 times a year	arba' marrāt fel sana	أربع مرات في السنة
date (e.g., today's ~)	tarīχ (m)	تاريخ
date (e.g., ~ of birth)	tarīχ (m)	تاريخ
calendar	natīga (f)	نتيجة
half a year	noṣṣ sana	نصّ سنة
six months	settet aʃ-hor (f)	ستّة أشهر
season (summer, etc.)	faṣl (m)	فصل
century	qarn (m)	قرن

TRAVEL. HOTEL

20. Trip. Travel

tourism, travel	seyāḥa (f)	سياحة
tourist	sā'eḥ (m)	سائح
trip, voyage	reḥla (f)	رحلة
adventure	moɣamra (f)	مغامرة
trip, journey	reḥla (f)	رحلة
vacation	agāza (f)	أجازة
to be on vacation	kān fi agāza	كان في أجازة
rest	estrāḥa (f)	إستراحة
train	qeṭār, 'aṭṭr (m)	قطار
by train	bel qeṭār - bel aṭṭr	بالقطار
airplane	ṭayāra (f)	طيّارة
by airplane	bel ṭayāra	بالطيّارة
by car	bel sayāra	بالسيّارة
by ship	bel safīna	بالسفينة
luggage	el ʃonaṭ (pl)	الشنط
suitcase	ʃanṭa (f)	شنطة
luggage cart	'arabet ʃonaṭ (f)	عربة شنط
passport	basbore (m)	باسبور
visa	ta'ʃīra (f)	تأشيرة
ticket	tazkara (f)	تذكرة
air ticket	tazkara ṭayarān (f)	تذكرة طيران
guidebook	dalīl (m)	دليل
map (tourist ~)	xarīṭa (f)	خريطة
area (rural ~)	mante'a (f)	منطقة
place, site	makān (m)	مكان
exotica (n)	ɣarāba (f)	غرابة
exotic (adj)	ɣarīb	غريب
amazing (adj)	mod-heʃ	مدهش
group	magmū'a (f)	مجموعة
excursion, sightseeing tour	gawla (f)	جولة
guide (person)	morʃed (m)	مرشد

21. Hotel

hotel	fondo' (m)	فندق
motel	motel (m)	موتيل
three-star (~ hotel)	talat nogūm	ثلاث نجوم
five-star	χamas nogūm	خمس نجوم
to stay (in a hotel, etc.)	nezel	نزل
room	oḍa (f)	أوضة
single room	owḍa le ʃaχṣ wāḥed (f)	أوضة لشخص واحد
double room	oḍa le ʃaχṣeyn (f)	أوضة لشخصين
to book a room	ḥagaz owḍa	حجز أوضة
half board	wagbeteyn fel yome (du)	وجبتين في اليوم
full board	talat wagabāt fel yome	ثلاث وجبات في اليوم
with bath	bel banyo	بـ البانيو
with shower	bel doʃ	بالدوش
satellite television	televizion be qanawāt faḍā'iya (m)	تليفزيون بقنوات فضائية
air-conditioner	takyīf (m)	تكييف
towel	fūṭa (f)	فوطة
key	meftāḥ (m)	مفتاح
administrator	modīr (m)	مدير
chambermaid	ʿāmela tandīf ɣoraf (f)	عاملة تنظيف غرف
porter, bellboy	ʃayāl (m)	شيّال
doorman	bawwāb (m)	بوّاب
restaurant	maṭʿam (m)	مطعم
pub, bar	bār (m)	بار
breakfast	foṭūr (m)	فطور
dinner	ʿaʃā' (m)	عشاء
buffet	bofeyh (m)	بوفيه
lobby	rad-ha (f)	ردهة
elevator	asanseyr (m)	اسانسير
DO NOT DISTURB	nargu ʿadam el ezʿāg	نرجو عدم الإزعاج
NO SMOKING	mamnūʿ el tadχīn	ممنوع التدخين

22. Sightseeing

monument	temsāl (m)	تمثال
fortress	'alʿa (f)	قلعة
palace	'aṣr (m)	قصر
castle	'alʿa (f)	قلعة
tower	borg (m)	برج

mausoleum	ḍarīḥ (m)	ضريح
architecture	handasa me'māriya (f)	هندسة معمارية
medieval (adj)	men el qorūn el wosṭa	من القرون الوسطى
ancient (adj)	'atīq	عتيق
national (adj)	waṭany	وطني
famous (monument, etc.)	maʃ-hūr	مشهور
tourist	sā'eḥ (m)	سائح
guide (person)	morʃed (m)	مرشد
excursion, sightseeing tour	gawla (f)	جولة
to show (vt)	warra	ورّى
to tell (vt)	'āl	قال
to find (vt)	la'a	لقى
to get lost (lose one's way)	ḍā'	ضاع
map (e.g., subway ~)	χarīṭa (f)	خريطة
map (e.g., city ~)	χarīṭa (f)	خريطة
souvenir, gift	tezkār (m)	تذكار
gift shop	maḥal hadāya (m)	محل هدايا
to take pictures	ṣawwar	صوّر
to have one's picture taken	etṣawwar	إتصوّر

TRANSPORTATION

23. Airport

airport	maṭār (m)	مطار
airplane	ṭayāra (f)	طيّارة
airline	ʃerket ṭayarān (f)	شركة طيران
air traffic controller	marākeb el ḥaraka el gawiya (m)	مراكب الحركة الجويّة
departure	moɣadra (f)	مغادرة
arrival	woṣūl (m)	وصول
to arrive (by plane)	weṣel	وصل
departure time	wa'tel moɣadra (m)	وقت المغادرة
arrival time	wa'tel woṣūl (m)	وقت الوصول
to be delayed	ta'akχar	تأخّر
flight delay	ta'aχor el reḥla (m)	تأخّر الرحلة
information board	lawḥet el ma'lomāt (f)	لوحة المعلومات
information	este'lamāt (pl)	إستعلامات
to announce (vt)	a'lan	أعلن
flight (e.g., next ~)	reḥlet ṭayarān (f)	رحلة طيران
customs	gamārek (pl)	جمارك
customs officer	mowazzaf el gamārek (m)	موظّف الجمارك
customs declaration	taṣrīḥ gomroky (m)	تصريح جمركي
to fill out (vt)	mala	ملا
to fill out the declaration	mala el taṣrīḥ	ملأ التصريح
passport control	taftīʃ el gawazāt (m)	تفتيش الجوازات
luggage	el ʃonaṭ (pl)	الشنط
hand luggage	ʃonaṭ el yad (pl)	شنط اليد
luggage cart	'arabet ʃonaṭ (f)	عربة شنط
landing	hobūṭ (m)	هبوط
landing strip	mamarr el hobūṭ (m)	ممرّ الهبوط
to land (vi)	habaṭ	هبط
airstairs	sellem el ṭayāra (m)	سلّم الطيّارة
check-in	tasgīl (m)	تسجيل
check-in counter	makān tasgīl (m)	مكان تسجيل
to check-in (vi)	saggel	سجّل
boarding pass	beṭāqet el rokūb (f)	بطاقة الركوب

departure gate	bawwābet el moɣadra (f)	بوّابة المغادرة
transit	tranzīt (m)	ترانزيت
to wait (vt)	estanna	إستنّى
departure lounge	ṣālet el moɣadra (f)	صالة المغادرة
to see off	wadda'	ودّع
to say goodbye	wadda'	ودّع

24. Airplane

airplane	ṭayāra (f)	طيّارة
air ticket	tazkara ṭayarān (f)	تذكرة طيران
airline	ʃerket ṭayarān (f)	شركة طيران
airport	maṭār (m)	مطار
supersonic (adj)	χāreq lel ṣote	خارق للصوت
captain	kabten (m)	كابتن
crew	ṭa'm (m)	طقم
pilot	ṭayār (m)	طيّار
flight attendant (fem.)	moḍīfet ṭayarān (f)	مضيفة طيران
navigator	mallāḥ (m)	ملّاح
wings	agneḥa (pl)	أجنحة
tail	deyl (m)	ذيل
cockpit	kabīna (f)	كابينة
engine	motore (m)	موتور
undercarriage (landing gear)	'agalāt el hobūṭ (pl)	عجلات الهبوط
turbine	torbīna (f)	توربينة
propeller	marwaḥa (f)	مروّحة
black box	mosaggel el ṭayarān (m)	مسجّل الطيران
yoke (control column)	moqawwed el ṭayāra (m)	مقوّد الطيّارة
fuel	woqūd (m)	وقود
safety card	beṭā'et el salāma (f)	بطاقة السلامة
oxygen mask	mask el oksyʒīn (m)	ماسك الاوكسيجين
uniform	zayī muwaḥḥad (m)	زيّ موحّد
life vest	sotret nagah (f)	سترة نجاة
parachute	baraʃot (m)	باراشوت
takeoff	eqlā' (m)	إقلاع
to take off (vi)	aqla'et	أقلعت
runway	modarrag el ṭa'erāṭ (m)	مدرّج الطائرات
visibility	ro'ya (f)	رؤية
flight (act of flying)	ṭayarān (m)	طيران
altitude	ertefā' (m)	إرتفاع
air pocket	geyb hawā'y (m)	جيب هوائي
seat	meq'ad (m)	مقعد
headphones	samma'āt ra'siya (pl)	سمّاعات رأسية

folding tray (tray table)	ṣeniya qabela lel ṭayī (f)	صينية قابلة للطيّ
airplane window	ʃebbāk el ṭayāra (m)	شبّاك الطيّارة
aisle	mamarr (m)	ممرّ

25. Train

train	qeṭār, 'aṭṭr (m)	قطار
commuter train	qeṭār rokkāb (m)	قطار ركّاب
express train	qeṭār saree' (m)	قطار سريع
diesel locomotive	qāṭeret dīzel (f)	قاطرة ديزل
steam locomotive	qāṭera boχariya (f)	قاطرة بخاريّة
passenger car	'araba (f)	عربة
dining car	'arabet el ṭa'ām (f)	عربة الطعام
rails	qoḍbān (pl)	قضبان
railroad	sekka ḥadīdiya (f)	سكّة حديديّة
railway tie	'āreḍa sekket ḥadīd (f)	عارضة سكّة الحديد
platform (railway ~)	raṣīf (m)	رصيف
track (~ 1, 2, etc.)	χaṭṭ (m)	خطّ
semaphore	semafore (m)	سيمافور
station	maḥaṭṭa (f)	محطّة
engineer (train driver)	sawwā' (m)	سوّاق
porter (of luggage)	ʃayāl (m)	شيّال
car attendant	mas'ūl 'arabet el qeṭār (m)	مسؤول عربة القطار
passenger	rākeb (m)	راكب
conductor (ticket inspector)	kamsary (m)	كمسري
corridor (in train)	mamarr (m)	ممرّ
emergency brake	farāmel el ṭawāre' (pl)	فرامل الطوارئ
compartment	ɣorfa (f)	غرفة
berth	serīr (m)	سرير
upper berth	serīr 'olwy (m)	سرير علوّي
lower berth	serīr sofly (m)	سرير سفلي
bed linen, bedding	aɣṭeyet el serīr (pl)	أغطيّة السرير
ticket	tazkara (f)	تذكرة
schedule	gadwal (m)	جدوّل
information display	lawḥet ma'lomāt (f)	لوحة معلومات
to leave, to depart	ɣādar	غادر
departure (of train)	moɣadra (f)	مغادرة
to arrive (ab. train)	weṣel	وصل
arrival	woṣūl (m)	وصول
to arrive by train	weṣel bel qeṭār	وصل بالقطار
to get on the train	rekeb el qeṭār	ركب القطار

to get off the train	nezel men el qeṭār	نزل من القطار
train wreck	ḥeṭām qeṭār (m)	حطام قطار
to derail (vi)	χarag ʿan χaṭṭ sīru	خرج عن خطّ سيره
steam locomotive	qāṭera boχariya (f)	قاطرة بخاريّة
stoker, fireman	ʿatʃagy (m)	عطشجي
firebox	forn el moḥarrek (m)	فرن المحرّك
coal	faḥm (m)	فحم

26. Ship

ship	safīna (f)	سفينة
vessel	safīna (f)	سفينة
steamship	baχera (f)	باخرة
riverboat	baχera nahriya (f)	باخرة نهرية
cruise ship	safīna seyaḥiya (f)	سفينة سياحيّة
cruiser	ṭarrād safīna baḥariya (m)	طرّاد سفينة بحريّة
yacht	yaχt (m)	يخت
tugboat	qāṭera baḥariya (f)	قاطرة بحريّة
barge	ṣandal (m)	صندل
ferry	ʿabbāra (f)	عبّارة
sailing ship	safīna ʃeraʿiya (m)	سفينة شراعيّة
brigantine	markeb ʃerāʿy (m)	مركب شراعي
ice breaker	moḥaṭṭemet galīd (f)	محطّمة جليد
submarine	ɣawwāṣa (f)	غوّاصة
boat (flat-bottomed ~)	markeb (m)	مركب
dinghy	zawraʾ (m)	زورق
lifeboat	qāreb nagah (m)	قارب نجاة
motorboat	lunʃ (m)	لنش
captain	ʾobṭān (m)	قبطان
seaman	baḥḥār (m)	بحّار
sailor	baḥḥār (m)	بحّار
crew	ṭāqem (m)	طاقم
boatswain	rabbān (m)	ربّان
ship's boy	ṣaby el safīna (m)	صبي السفينة
cook	ṭabbāχ (m)	طبّاخ
ship's doctor	ṭabīb el safīna (m)	طبيب السفينة
deck	saṭ-ḥ el safīna (m)	سطح السفينة
mast	sāreya (f)	سارية
sail	ʃerāʿ (m)	شراع
hold	ʿanbar (m)	عنبر
bow (prow)	moʾaddema (m)	مقدّمة

stern	mo'aχeret el safīna (f)	مؤخّرة السفينة
oar	megdāf (m)	مجذاف
screw propeller	marwaḥa (f)	مروّحة
cabin	kabīna (f)	كابينة
wardroom	ɣorfet el ṭa'ām wel rāḥa (f)	غرفة الطعام والراحة
engine room	qesm el 'ālāt (m)	قسم الآلات
bridge	borg el qeyāda (m)	برج القيادة
radio room	ɣorfet el lāselky (f)	غرفة اللاسلكي
wave (radio)	mouga (f)	موجة
logbook	segel el safīna (m)	سجل السفينة
spyglass	monzār (m)	منظار
bell	garas (m)	جرس
flag	'alam (m)	علم
hawser (mooring ~)	ḥabl (m)	حبل
knot (bowline, etc.)	'o'da (f)	عقدة
deckrails	drabzīn saṭ-ḥ el safīna (m)	درابزين سطح السفينة
gangway	sellem (m)	سلّم
anchor	marsāh (f)	مرساة
to weigh anchor	rafa' morsah	رفع مرساة
to drop anchor	rasa	رسا
anchor chain	selselet morsah (f)	سلسلة مرساة
port (harbor)	minā' (m)	ميناء
quay, wharf	marsa (m)	مرسى
to berth (moor)	rasa	رسا
to cast off	aqla'	أقلع
trip, voyage	reḥla (f)	رحلة
cruise (sea trip)	reḥla baḥariya (f)	رحلة بحريّة
course (route)	masār (m)	مسار
route (itinerary)	ṭarī' (m)	طريق
fairway (safe water channel)	magra melāḥy (m)	مجرى ملاحيّ
shallows	meyāh ḍaḥla (f)	مياه ضحلة
to run aground	ganaḥ	جنح
storm	'āṣefa (f)	عاصفة
signal	eʃara (f)	إشارة
to sink (vi)	ɣere'	غرق
Man overboard!	sa'aṭ rāgil min el sefīna!	سقط راجل من السفينة!
SOS (distress signal)	nedā' eɣāsa (m)	نداء إغاثة
ring buoy	ṭo'e nagah (m)	طوق نجاة

CITY

27. Urban transportation

bus	buṣ (m)	باص
streetcar	trām (m)	ترام
trolley bus	trolly buṣ (m)	ترولي باص
route (of bus, etc.)	χaṭṭ (m)	خطّ
number (e.g., bus ~)	raqam (m)	رقم
to go by ...	rāḥ be ...	... راح بـ
to get on (~ the bus)	rekeb	ركب
to get off ...	nezel men	نزل من
stop (e.g., bus ~)	maw'af (m)	موّقف
next stop	el maḥaṭṭa el gaya (f)	المحطة الجاية
terminus	'āχer maw'af (m)	آخر موقف
schedule	gadwal (m)	جدوَل
to wait (vt)	estanna	إستنّى
ticket	tazkara (f)	تذكرة
fare	ogra (f)	أجرة
cashier (ticket seller)	kaʃier (m)	كاشيير
ticket inspection	taftīʃ el tazāker (m)	تفتيش التذاكر
ticket inspector	mofatteʃ tazāker (m)	مفتّش تذاكر
to be late (for ...)	met'akχer	متأخّر
to miss (~ the train, etc.)	ta'akχar	تأخّر
to be in a hurry	mesta'gel	مستعجل
taxi, cab	taksi (m)	تاكسي
taxi driver	sawwā' taksi (m)	سوّاق تاكسي
by taxi	bel taksi	بالتاكسي
taxi stand	maw'ef taksi (m)	موّقف تاكسي
to call a taxi	kallem taksi	كلّم تاكسي
to take a taxi	aχad taksi	أخد تاكسي
traffic	ḥaraket el morūr (f)	حركة المرور
traffic jam	zaḥmet el morūr (f)	زحمة المرور
rush hour	sā'et el zorwa (f)	ساعة الذروة
to park (vi)	rakan	ركن
to park (vt)	rakan	ركن
parking lot	maw'ef el 'arabeyāt (m)	موقف العربيات
subway	metro (m)	مترو
station	maḥaṭṭa (f)	محطّة

to take the subway	aχad el metro	أخد المترو
train	qeṭār, ʾaṭṭr (m)	قطار
train station	maḥaṭṭet qeṭār (f)	محطّة قطار

28. City. Life in the city

city, town	madīna (f)	مدينة
capital city	ʿāṣema (f)	عاصمة
village	qarya (f)	قرية
city map	χarīṭet el madinah (f)	خريطة المدينة
downtown	wesṭ el balad (m)	وسط البلد
suburb	ḍāḥeya (f)	ضاحية
suburban (adj)	el ḍawāḥy	الضواحي
outskirts	aṭrāf el madīna (pl)	أطراف المدينة
environs (suburbs)	ḍawāḥy el madīna (pl)	ضواحي المدينة
city block	ḥayī (m)	حي
residential block (area)	ḥayī sakany (m)	حي سكني
traffic	ḥaraket el morūr (f)	حركة المرور
traffic lights	eʃārāt el morūr (pl)	إشارات المرور
public transportation	wasāʾel el naʾl (pl)	وسائل النقل
intersection	taqāṭoʿ (m)	تقاطع
crosswalk	maʿbar (m)	معبر
pedestrian underpass	nafaʾ moʃāh (m)	نفق مشاه
to cross (~ the street)	ʿabar	عبر
pedestrian	māʃy (m)	ماشي
sidewalk	raṣīf (m)	رصيف
bridge	kobry (m)	كبري
embankment (river walk)	korneyʃ (m)	كورنيش
fountain	nafūra (f)	نافورة
allée (garden walkway)	mamʃa (m)	ممشى
park	ḥadīqa (f)	حديقة
boulevard	bolvār (m)	بولفار
square	medān (m)	ميدان
avenue (wide street)	ʃāreʿ (m)	شارع
street	ʃāreʿ (m)	شارع
side street	zoʾāʾ (m)	زقاق
dead end	ṭarīʾ masdūd (m)	طريق مسدود
house	beyt (m)	بيت
building	mabna (m)	مبنى
skyscraper	nāṭeḥet sahāb (f)	ناطحة سحاب
facade	waɣa (f)	واجهة
roof	saʾf (m)	سقف

window	ʃebbāk (m)	شبّاك
arch	qose (m)	قوس
column	ʿamūd (m)	عمود
corner	zawya (f)	زاوية
store window	vatrīna (f)	فترينة
signboard (store sign, etc.)	yafṭa, lāfeta (f)	لافتة, يافطة
poster	boster (m)	بوستر
advertising poster	boster eʿlān (m)	بوستر إعلان
billboard	lawḥet eʿlanāt (f)	لوحة إعلانات
garbage, trash	zebāla (f)	زبالة
trashcan (public ~)	ṣandūʾ zebāla (m)	صندوق زبالة
to litter (vi)	rama zebāla	رمى زبالة
garbage dump	mazbala (f)	مزبلة
phone booth	koʃk telefōn (m)	كشك تليفون
lamppost	ʿamūd nūr (m)	عمود نور
bench (park ~)	korsy (m)	كرسي
police officer	ʃorṭy (m)	شرطي
police	ʃorṭa (f)	شرطة
beggar	ʃaḥḥāt (m)	شحّات
homeless (n)	motaʃarred (m)	متشرّد

29. Urban institutions

store	maḥal (m)	محل
drugstore, pharmacy	ṣaydaliya (f)	صيدليّة
eyeglass store	maḥal naḍḍārāt (m)	محل نضّارات
shopping mall	mole (m)	مول
supermarket	subermarket (m)	سوبرماركت
bakery	maχbaz (m)	مخبز
baker	χabbāz (m)	خبّاز
pastry shop	ḥalawāny (m)	حلواني
grocery store	baʾʾāla (f)	بقّالة
butcher shop	gezāra (f)	جزارة
produce store	dokkān χoḍār (m)	دكّان خضار
market	sūʾ (f)	سوق
coffee house	ʾahwa (f), kaféih (m)	قهوة, كافيه
restaurant	maṭʿam (m)	مطعم
pub, bar	bār (m)	بار
pizzeria	maḥal pizza (m)	محل بيتزا
hair salon	ṣalone ḥelāʾa (m)	صالون حلاقة
post office	maktab el barīd (m)	مكتب البريد
dry cleaners	dray klīn (m)	دراي كلين

photo studio	estudio taṣwīr (m)	إستوديو تصوير
shoe store	maḥal gezam (m)	محل جزم
bookstore	maḥal kotob (m)	محل كتب
sporting goods store	maḥal mostalzamāt reyaḍiya (m)	محل مستلزمات رياضية
clothes repair shop	maḥal χeyāṭet malābes (m)	محل خياطة ملابس
formal wear rental	ta'gīr malābes rasmiya (m)	تأجير ملابس رسمية
video rental store	maḥal ta'gīr video (m)	محل تأجير فيديو
circus	serk (m)	سيرك
zoo	ḥadīqet el ḥayawān (f)	حديقة حيوان
movie theater	sinema (f)	سينما
museum	mat-ḥaf (m)	متحف
library	maktaba (f)	مكتبة
theater	masraḥ (m)	مسرح
opera (opera house)	obra (f)	أوبرا
nightclub	malha leyly (m)	ملهى ليّلي
casino	kazino (m)	كازينو
mosque	masged (m)	مسجد
synagogue	kenīs (m)	كنيس
cathedral	katedra'iya (f)	كاتدرائية
temple	ma'bad (m)	معبد
church	kenīsa (f)	كنيسة
college	kolliya (m)	كلّية
university	gam'a (f)	جامعة
school	madrasa (f)	مدرسة
prefecture	moqaṭ'a (f)	مقاطعة
city hall	baladiya (f)	بلديّة
hotel	fondo' (m)	فندق
bank	bank (m)	بنك
embassy	safāra (f)	سفارة
travel agency	ʃerket seyāḥa (f)	شركة سياحة
information office	maktab el este'lāmāt (m)	مكتب الإستعلامات
currency exchange	ṣarrāfa (f)	صرّافة
subway	metro (m)	مترو
hospital	mostaʃfa (m)	مستشفى
gas station	maḥaṭṭet banzīn (f)	محطّة بنزين
parking lot	maw'ef el 'arabeyāt (m)	موقف العربيات

30. Signs

signboard (store sign, etc.)	yafṭa, lāfeta (f)	لافتة, يافطة
notice (door sign, etc.)	bayān (m)	بيان

poster	boster (m)	بوستر
direction sign	'alāmet (f)	علامة إتجاه
arrow (sign)	'alāmet eʃāra (f)	علامة إشارة
caution	taḥzīr (m)	تحذير
warning sign	lāfetat taḥzīr (f)	لافتة تحذير
to warn (vt)	ḥazzar	حذّر
rest day (weekly ~)	yome 'oṭla (m)	يوم عطلة
timetable (schedule)	gadwal (m)	جدوّل
opening hours	aw'āt el 'amal (pl)	أوقات العمل
WELCOME!	ahlan w sahlan!	!أهلاً وسهلا
ENTRANCE	doχūl	دخول
EXIT	χorūg	خروج
PUSH	edfa'	إدفع
PULL	es-ḥab	إسحب
OPEN	maftūḥ	مفتوح
CLOSED	moɣlaq	مغلق
WOMEN	lel sayedāt	للسيدات
MEN	lel regāl	للرجال
DISCOUNTS	χoṣomāt	خصومات
SALE	taχfeḍāt	تخفيضات
NEW!	gedīd!	!جديد
FREE	maggānan	مجّاناً
ATTENTION!	entebāh!	!إنتباه
NO VACANCIES	koll el amāken maḥgūza	كلّ الأماكن محجوزة
RESERVED	maḥgūz	محجوز
ADMINISTRATION	edāra	إدارة
STAFF ONLY	lel 'amelīn faqaṭ	للعاملين فقط
BEWARE OF THE DOG!	eḥzar wogūd kalb	إحذر وجود الكلب
NO SMOKING	mamnū' el tadχīn	ممنوع التدخين
DO NOT TOUCH!	'adam el lams	عدم اللمس
DANGEROUS	χaṭīr	خطير
DANGER	χaṭar	خطر
HIGH VOLTAGE	tayār 'āly	تيّار عالي
NO SWIMMING!	el sebāḥa mamnū'a	السباحة ممنوعة
OUT OF ORDER	mo'aṭṭal	معطّل
FLAMMABLE	saree' el eʃte'āl	سريع الإشتعال
FORBIDDEN	mamnū'	ممنوع
NO TRESPASSING!	mamnū' el morūr	ممنوع المرور
WET PAINT	eḥzar ṭelā' ɣayr gāf	احذر طلاء غير جاف

31. Shopping

to buy (purchase)	eʃtara	إشترى
purchase	ḥāga (f)	حاجة
to go shopping	eʃtara	إشترى
shopping	ʃobbing (m)	شوبينج
to be open (ab. store)	maftūḥ	مفتوح
to be closed	moɣlaq	مغلق
footwear, shoes	gezam (pl)	جزم
clothes, clothing	malābes (pl)	ملابس
cosmetics	mawād tagmīl (pl)	مواد تجميل
food products	akl (m)	أكل
gift, present	hediya (f)	هديّة
salesman	bayā‘ (m)	بيّاع
saleswoman	bayā‘a (f)	بيّاعة
check out, cash desk	ṣandū’ el daf‘ (m)	صندوق الدفع
mirror	merāya (f)	مراية
counter (store ~)	manḍada (f)	منضدة
fitting room	ɣorfet el ’eyās (f)	غرفة القياس
to try on	garrab	جرّب
to fit (ab. dress, etc.)	nāseb	ناسب
to like (I like ...)	‘agab	عجب
price	se‘r (m)	سعر
price tag	tiket el se‘r (m)	تيكت السعر
to cost (vt)	kallef	كلّف
How much?	bekām?	بكام؟
discount	χaṣm (m)	خصم
inexpensive (adj)	meʃ ɣāly	مش غالي
cheap (adj)	reχīṣ	رخيص
expensive (adj)	ɣāly	غالي
It's expensive	da ɣāly	ده غالي
rental (n)	este’gār (m)	إستئجار
to rent (~ a tuxedo)	est’gar	إستأجر
credit (trade credit)	e’temān (m)	إئتمان
on credit (adv)	bel ta’seeṭ	بالتقسيط

CLOTHING & ACCESSORIES

32. Outerwear. Coats

clothes	malābes (pl)	ملابس
outerwear	malābes fo'aniya (pl)	ملابس فوقانيّة
winter clothing	malābes ʃetwiya (pl)	ملابس شتويّة
coat (overcoat)	balṭo (m)	بالطو
fur coat	balṭo farww (m)	بالطو فروّ
fur jacket	ʒaket farww (m)	جاكيت فروّ
down coat	balṭo maḥʃy rīʃ (m)	بالطو محشي ريش
jacket (e.g., leather ~)	ʒæket (m)	جاكيت
raincoat (trenchcoat, etc.)	ʒæket lel maṭar (m)	جاكيت للمطر
waterproof (adj)	wāqy men el maya	واقي من الميّة

33. Men's & women's clothing

shirt (button shirt)	'amīṣ (m)	قميص
pants	banṭalone (f)	بنطلون
jeans	ʒeans (m)	جينز
suit jacket	ʒæket (f)	جاكت
suit	badla (f)	بدلة
dress (frock)	fostān (m)	فستان
skirt	ʒība (f)	جيبة
blouse	bloza (f)	بلوزة
knitted jacket (cardigan, etc.)	kardigan (m)	كارديجن
jacket (of woman's suit)	ʒæket (m)	جاكيت
T-shirt	ti ʃirt (m)	تي شيرت
shorts (short trousers)	ʃort (m)	شورت
tracksuit	treneng (m)	ترينينج
bathrobe	robe el ḥammām (m)	روب حمّام
pajamas	beʒāma (f)	بيجاما
sweater	blover (f)	بلوفر
pullover	blover (m)	بلوفر
vest	vest (m)	فيست
tailcoat	badlet sahra ṭawīla (f)	بدلة سهرة طويلة
tuxedo	badla (f)	بدلة

uniform	zayī muwaḥḥad (m)	زيّ موحّد
workwear	lebs el ʃoɣl (m)	لبس الشغل
overalls	overall (m)	اوفر اول
coat (e.g., doctor's smock)	balṭo (m)	بالطو

34. Clothing. Underwear

underwear	malābes dāχeliya (pl)	ملابس داخلية
boxers, briefs	sirwāl dāχly rigāly (m)	سروال داخلي رجاليّ
panties	sirwāl dāχly nisā'y (m)	سروال داخلي نسائيّ
undershirt (A-shirt)	fanella (f)	فانلّا
socks	ʃarāb (m)	شراب
nightgown	'amīṣ nome (m)	قميص نوم
bra	setyāna (f)	ستيانة
knee highs (knee-high socks)	ʃarabāt ṭawīla (pl)	شرابات طويلة
pantyhose	klone (m)	كلون
stockings (thigh highs)	gawāreb (pl)	جوارب
bathing suit	mayo (m)	مايّوه

35. Headwear

hat	ṭa'iya (f)	طاقيّة
fedora	borneyṭa (f)	برنيطة
baseball cap	base bāl kāb (m)	بيس بول كاب
flatcap	ṭa'iya mosaṭṭaḥa (f)	طاقيّة مسطحة
beret	bereyh (m)	بيريه
hood	ɣaṭa' (f)	غطاء
panama hat	qobba'et banama (f)	قبّعة بناما
knit cap (knitted hat)	ays kāb (m)	آيس كاب
headscarf	eʃarb (m)	إيشارب
women's hat	borneyṭa (f)	برنيطة
hard hat	χawza (f)	خوذة
garrison cap	kāb (m)	كاب
helmet	χawza (f)	خوذة
derby	qobba'a (f)	قبّعة
top hat	qobba'a rasmiya (f)	قبّعة رسمية

36. Footwear

footwear	gezam (pl)	جزم
shoes (men's shoes)	gazma (f)	جزمة

shoes (women's shoes)	gazma (f)	جزمة
boots (e.g., cowboy ~)	būt (m)	بوت
slippers	ʃebʃeb (m)	شبشب
tennis shoes (e.g., Nike ~)	kotʃy tennis (m)	كوتشي تنس
sneakers (e.g., Converse ~)	kotʃy (m)	كوتشي
sandals	ṣandal (pl)	صندل
cobbler (shoe repairer)	eskāfy (m)	إسكافي
heel	kaʿb (m)	كعب
pair (of shoes)	goze (m)	جوز
shoestring	ʃerīʾṭ (m)	شريط
to lace (vt)	rabaṭ	ربط
shoehorn	labbāsa el gazma (f)	لبّاسة الجزمة
shoe polish	warnīʃ el gazma (m)	ورنيش الجزمة

37. Personal accessories

gloves	gwanty (m)	جوانتي
mittens	gwanty men ɣeyr aṣābeʿ (m)	جوانتي من غير أصابع
scarf (muffler)	skarf (m)	سكارف
glasses (eyeglasses)	naḍḍāra (f)	نظّارة
frame (eyeglass ~)	eṭār (m)	إطار
umbrella	ʃamsiya (f)	شمسيّة
walking stick	ʿaṣāya (f)	عصاية
hairbrush	forʃet ʃaʿr (f)	فرشة شعر
fan	marwaḥa (f)	مروّحة
tie (necktie)	karavetta (f)	كرافتة
bow tie	bebyona (m)	بيبيونة
suspenders	ḥammala (f)	حمّالة
handkerchief	mandīl (m)	منديل
comb	meʃṭ (m)	مشط
barrette	dabbūs (m)	دبّوس
hairpin	bensa (m)	بنسة
buckle	bokla (f)	بكلة
belt	ḥezām (m)	حزام
shoulder strap	ḥammalet el ketf (f)	حمّالة الكتف
bag (handbag)	ʃanṭa (f)	شنطة
purse	ʃanṭet yad (f)	شنطة يد
backpack	ʃanṭet ḍahr (f)	شنطة ظهر

38. Clothing. Miscellaneous

fashion	mūḍa (f)	موضة
in vogue (adj)	fel moḍa	في الموضة
fashion designer	moṣammem azyā' (m)	مصمّم أزياء
collar	yā'a (f)	ياقة
pocket	geyb (m)	جيب
pocket (as adj)	geyb	جيب
sleeve	komm (m)	كمّ
hanging loop	'elāqa (f)	علّاقة
fly (on trousers)	lesān (m)	لسان
zipper (fastener)	sosta (f)	سوستة
fastener	maʃbak (m)	مشبك
button	zerr (m)	زرّ
buttonhole	'arwa (f)	عروة
to come off (ab. button)	we'e'	وقع
to sew (vi, vt)	χayaṭ	خيّط
to embroider (vi, vt)	ṭarraz	طرّز
embroidery	taṭrīz (m)	تطريز
sewing needle	ebra (f)	إبرة
thread	χeyṭ (m)	خيط
seam	derz (m)	درز
to get dirty (vi)	ettwassaχ	إتّوسّخ
stain (mark, spot)	bo''a (f)	بقعة
to crease, crumple (vi)	takarmaʃ	تكرمش
to tear, to rip (vt)	'aṭa'	قطع
clothes moth	'etta (f)	عثّة

39. Personal care. Cosmetics

toothpaste	ma'gūn asnān (m)	معجون أسنان
toothbrush	forʃet senān (f)	فرشة أسنان
to brush one's teeth	naḍḍaf el asnān	نظّف الأسنان
razor	mūs (m)	موس
shaving cream	krīm ḥelā'a (m)	كريم حلاقة
to shave (vi)	ḥala'	حلق
soap	ṣabūn (m)	صابون
shampoo	ʃambū (m)	شامبو
scissors	ma'aṣ (m)	مقص
nail file	mabrad (m)	مبرد
nail clippers	mel'aṭ (m)	ملقط
tweezers	mel'aṭ (m)	ملقط

cosmetics	mawād tagmīl (pl)	مواد تجميل
face mask	mask (m)	ماسك
manicure	monekīr (m)	مونيكير
to have a manicure	'amal monikīr	عمل مونيكير
pedicure	badikīr (m)	باديكير
make-up bag	ʃanṭet mekyāʒ (f)	شنطة مكياج
face powder	bodret weʃ (f)	بودرة وش
powder compact	'elbet bodra (f)	علبة بودرة
blusher	aḥmar χodūd (m)	أحمر خدود
perfume (bottled)	barfān (m)	بارفان
toilet water (lotion)	kolonya (f)	كولونيا
lotion	loʃion (m)	لوشن
cologne	kolonya (f)	كولونيا
eyeshadow	eyeʃadow (m)	ايّ شادو
eyeliner	koḥl (m)	كحل
mascara	maskara (f)	ماسكارا
lipstick	rūʒ (m)	روج
nail polish, enamel	monekīr (m)	مونيكير
hair spray	mosabbet el ʃa'r (m)	مثبّت الشعر
deodorant	mozīl 'ara' (m)	مزيل عرق
cream	krīm (m)	كريم
face cream	krīm lel weʃ (m)	كريم للوش
hand cream	krīm eyd (m)	كريم أيد
anti-wrinkle cream	krīm moḍād lel taga'īd (m)	كريم مضاد للتجاعيد
day cream	krīm en nahār (m)	كريم النهار
night cream	krīm el leyl (m)	كريم الليل
day (as adj)	nahāry	نهاري
night (as adj)	layly	ليّلي
tampon	tambon (m)	تانبون
toilet paper (toilet roll)	wara' twalet (m)	ورق تواليت
hair dryer	seʃwār (m)	سشوار

40. Watches. Clocks

watch (wristwatch)	sā'a (f)	ساعة
dial	wag-h el sā'a (m)	وجه الساعة
hand (of clock, watch)	'a'rab el sā'a (m)	عقرب الساعة
metal watch band	ʃerī'ṭ sā'a ma'daniya (m)	شريط ساعة معدنية
watch strap	ʃerī'ṭ el sā'a (m)	شريط الساعة
battery	baṭṭariya (f)	بطّاريّة
to be dead (battery)	χelṣet	خلصت
to change a battery	ɣayar el baṭṭariya	غيّر البطّاريّة
to run fast	saba'	سبق

to run slow	ta'akχar	تأخّر
wall clock	sā'et ḥeyṭa (f)	ساعة حيطة
hourglass	sā'a ramliya (f)	ساعة رمليّة
sundial	sā'a ʃamsiya (f)	ساعة شمسيّة
alarm clock	monabbeh (m)	منبّه
watchmaker	sa'āty (m)	ساعاتي
to repair (vt)	ṣallaḥ	صلّح

EVERYDAY EXPERIENCE

41. Money

money	folūs (pl)	فلوس
currency exchange	taḥwīl 'omla (m)	تحويل عملة
exchange rate	se'r el ṣarf (m)	سعر الصرف
ATM	makinet ṣarrāf 'āly (f)	ماكينة صرّاف آلي
coin	'erʃ (m)	قرش
dollar	dolār (m)	دولار
euro	yoro (m)	يورو
lira	lira (f)	ليرة
Deutschmark	el mark el almāny (m)	المارك الألماني
franc	frank (m)	فرنك
pound sterling	geneyh esterlīny (m)	جنيه استرليني
yen	yen (m)	ين
debt	deyn (m)	دين
debtor	modīn (m)	مدين
to lend (money)	sallef	سلّف
to borrow (vi, vt)	estalaf	إستلف
bank	bank (m)	بنك
account	ḥesāb (m)	حساب
to deposit (vt)	awda'	أودع
to deposit into the account	awda' fel ḥesāb	أودّع في الحساب
to withdraw (vt)	saḥab men el ḥesāb	سحب من الحساب
credit card	kredit kard (f)	كريدت كارد
cash	kæʃ (m)	كاش
check	ʃīk (m)	شيك
to write a check	katab ʃīk	كتب شيك
checkbook	daftar ʃikāt (m)	دفتر شيكات
wallet	maḥfaẓa (f)	محفظة
change purse	maḥfazet fakka (f)	محفظة فكّة
safe	χazzāna (f)	خزّانة
heir	wāres (m)	وارث
inheritance	werāsa (f)	وراثة
fortune (wealth)	sarwa (f)	ثروّة
lease	'a'd el egār (m)	عقد الإيجار
rent (money)	ogret el sakan (f)	أجرة السكن

to rent (sth from sb)	est'gar	إستأجر
price	se'r (m)	سعر
cost	taman (m)	ثمن
sum	mablay (m)	مبلغ
to spend (vt)	ṣaraf	صرف
expenses	maṣarīf (pl)	مصاريف
to economize (vi, vt)	waffar	وفّر
economical	mowaffer	موّفر
to pay (vi, vt)	dafa'	دفع
payment	daf' (m)	دفع
change (give the ~)	el bā'y (m)	الباقي
tax	ḍarība (f)	ضريبة
fine	ɣarāma (f)	غرامة
to fine (vt)	faraḍ ɣarāma	فرض غرامة

42. Post. Postal service

post office	maktab el barīd (m)	مكتب البريد
mail (letters, etc.)	el barīd (m)	البريد
mailman	sā'y el barīd (m)	ساعي البريد
opening hours	aw'āt el 'amal (pl)	أوقات العمل
letter	resāla (f)	رسالة
registered letter	resāla mosaggala (f)	رسالة مسجّلة
postcard	kart barīdy (m)	كرت بريدي
telegram	barqiya (f)	برقيّة
package (parcel)	ṭard (m)	طرد
money transfer	ḥewāla māliya (f)	حوالة مالية
to receive (vt)	estalam	إستلم
to send (vt)	arsal	أرسل
sending	ersāl (m)	إرسال
address	'enwān (m)	عنوان
ZIP code	raqam el barīd (m)	رقم البريد
sender	morsel (m)	مرسل
receiver	morsel elayh (m)	مرسل إليه
name (first name)	esm (m)	اسم
surname (last name)	esm el 'a'ela (m)	اسم العائلة
postage rate	ta'rīfa (f)	تعريفة
standard (adj)	'ādy	عادي
economical (adj)	mowaffer	موّفر
weight	wazn (m)	وزن
to weigh (~ letters)	wazan	وزن

envelope	ẓarf (m)	ظرف
postage stamp	ṭābeʿ (m)	طابع
to stamp an envelope	alṣaq ṭābeʿ	ألصق طابع

43. Banking

bank	bank (m)	بنك
branch (of bank, etc.)	farʿ (m)	فرع
bank clerk, consultant	mowazzaf bank (m)	موظّف بنك
manager (director)	modīr (m)	مدير
bank account	ḥesāb bank (m)	حساب بنك
account number	raqam el ḥesāb (m)	رقم الحساب
checking account	ḥesāb gāry (m)	حساب جاري
savings account	ḥesāb tawfīr (m)	حساب توّفير
to open an account	fataḥ ḥesāb	فتح حساب
to close the account	ʾafal ḥesāb	قفل حساب
to deposit into the account	awdaʿ fel ḥesāb	أودع في الحساب
to withdraw (vt)	saḥab men el ḥesāb	سحب من الحساب
deposit	wadeeʿa (f)	وديعة
to make a deposit	awdaʿ	أودع
wire transfer	ḥewāla maṣrefiya (f)	حوالة مصرفيّة
to wire, to transfer	ḥawwel	حوّل
sum	mablaɣ (m)	مبلغ
How much?	kām?	كام؟
signature	tawqeeʿ (m)	توقيع
to sign (vt)	waqqaʿ	وقّع
credit card	kredit kard (f)	كريدت كارد
code (PIN code)	kōd (m)	كود
credit card number	raqam el kredit kard (m)	رقم الكريدت كارد
ATM	makinet ṣarrāf ʾāly (f)	ماكينة صرّاف آلي
check	ʃīk (m)	شيك
to write a check	katab ʃīk	كتب شيك
checkbook	daftar ʃikāt (m)	دفتر شيكات
loan (bank ~)	qarḍ (m)	قرض
to apply for a loan	ʾaddem ṭalab ʿala qarḍ	قدّم طلب على قرض
to get a loan	ḥaṣal ʿala qarḍ	حصل على قرض
to give a loan	edda qarḍ	ادّى قرض
guarantee	ḍamān (m)	ضمان

44. Telephone. Phone conversation

telephone	telefon (m)	تليفون
cell phone	mobile (m)	موبايل
answering machine	gehāz radd 'alal mokalmāt (m)	جهاز ردّ على المكالمات
to call (by phone)	ettaṣal	إتّصل
phone call	mokalma telefoniya (f)	مكالمة تليفونية
to dial a number	ettaṣal be raqam	إتّصل برقم
Hello!	alo!	ألو!
to ask (vt)	sa'al	سأل
to answer (vi, vt)	radd	ردّ
to hear (vt)	seme'	سمع
well (adv)	kewayes	كويّس
not well (adv)	meʃ kowayīs	مش كويّس
noises (interference)	taʃwīʃ (m)	تشويش
receiver	sammā'a (f)	سمّاعة
to pick up (~ the phone)	rafa' el sammā'a	رفع السمّاعة
to hang up (~ the phone)	'afal el sammā'a	قفل السمّاعة
busy (engaged)	maʃɣūl	مشغول
to ring (ab. phone)	rann	رنّ
telephone book	dalīl el telefone (m)	دليل التليفون
local (adj)	maḥalliyya	ة محلّيّة
local call	mokalma maḥalliya (f)	مكالمة محلّيّة
long distance (~ call)	bi'īd	بعيد
long-distance call	mokalma bi'īda (f)	مكالمة بعيدة المدى
international (adj)	dowly	دوّلي
international call	mokalma dowliya (f)	مكالمة دوليّة

45. Cell phone

cell phone	mobile (m)	موبايل
display	'arḍ (m)	عرض
button	zerr (m)	زرّ
SIM card	sim kard (m)	سيم كارد
battery	baṭṭariya (f)	بطّاريّة
to be dead (battery)	χelṣet	خلصت
charger	ʃāḥen (m)	شاحن
menu	qā'ema (f)	قائمة
settings	awḍā' (pl)	أوضاع
tune (melody)	naɣama (f)	نغمة

to select (vt)	eχtār	إختار
calculator	'āla ḥasba (f)	آلة حاسبة
voice mail	barīd ṣawty (m)	بريد صوتي
alarm clock	monabbeh (m)	منبّه
contacts	gehāt el etteṣāl (pl)	جهات الإتّصال
SMS (text message)	resāla 'aṣīra ɛsɛmɛs (f)	رسالة قصيرة sms
subscriber	moʃtarek (m)	مشترك

46. Stationery

ballpoint pen	'alam gāf (m)	قلم جاف
fountain pen	'alam rīʃa (m)	قلم ريشة
pencil	'alam roṣāṣ (m)	قلم رصاص
highlighter	markar (m)	ماركر
felt-tip pen	'alam fulumaster (m)	قلم فلوماستر
notepad	mozakkera (f)	مذكّرة
agenda (diary)	gadwal el a'māl (m)	جدول الأعمال
ruler	masṭara (f)	مسطرة
calculator	'āla ḥasba (f)	آلة حاسبة
eraser	astīka (f)	استيكة
thumbtack	dabbūs (m)	دبّوس
paper clip	dabbūs wara' (m)	دبّوس ورق
glue	ṣamɣ (m)	صمغ
stapler	dabbāsa (f)	دبّاسة
hole punch	χarrāma (m)	خرّامة
pencil sharpener	barrāya (f)	برّاية

47. Foreign languages

language	loɣa (f)	لغة
foreign (adj)	agnaby	أجنبيّ
foreign language	loɣa agnabiya (f)	لغة أجنبية
to study (vt)	daras	درس
to learn (language, etc.)	ta'allam	تعلّم
to read (vi, vt)	'ara	قرأ
to speak (vi, vt)	kallem	كلّم
to understand (vt)	fehem	فهم
to write (vt)	katab	كتب
fast (adv)	bosor'a	بسرعة
slowly (adv)	bo boṭ'	ببطء
fluently (adv)	beṭalāqa	بطلاقة

rules	qawā'ed (pl)	قواعد
grammar	el naḥw wel ṣarf (m)	النحو والصرف
vocabulary	mofradāt el loɣa (pl)	مفردات اللغة
phonetics	ṣawtīāt (pl)	صوتيات
textbook	ketāb ta'līm (m)	كتاب تعليم
dictionary	qamūs (m)	قاموس
teach-yourself book	ketāb ta'līm zāty (m)	كتاب تعليم ذاتي
phrasebook	ketāb lel 'ebarāt el ʃā'e'a (m)	كتاب للعبارت الشائعة
cassette, tape	kasett (m)	كاسيت
videotape	ʃerī'ṭ video (m)	شريط فيديو
CD, compact disc	sidī (m)	سي دي
DVD	dividī (m)	دي في دي
alphabet	abgadiya (f)	أبجدية
to spell (vt)	tahagga	تهجّى
pronunciation	noṭ' (m)	نطق
accent	lahga (f)	لهجة
with an accent	be lahga	بـ لهجة
without an accent	men ɣeyr lahga	من غير لهجة
word	kelma (f)	كلمة
meaning	ma'na (m)	معنى
course (e.g., a French ~)	dawra (f)	دورة
to sign up	saggel esmo	سجّل إسمه
teacher	modarres (m)	مدرس
translation (process)	targama (f)	ترجمة
translation (text, etc.)	targama (f)	ترجمة
translator	motargem (m)	مترجم
interpreter	motargem fawwry (m)	مترجم فوّري
polyglot	'alīm be'eddet loɣāt (m)	عليم بعدّة لغات
memory	zākera (f)	ذاكرة

MEALS. RESTAURANT

48. Table setting

spoon	ma'la'a (f)	معلقة
knife	sekkīna (f)	سكّينة
fork	ʃawka (f)	شوكة
cup (e.g., coffee ~)	fengān (m)	فنجان
plate (dinner ~)	ṭaba' (m)	طبق
saucer	ṭaba' fengān (m)	طبق فنجان
napkin (on table)	mandīl wara' (m)	منديل ورق
toothpick	χallet senān (f)	خلة سنان

49. Restaurant

restaurant	maṭ'am (m)	مطعم
coffee house	'ahwa (f), kaféih (m)	قهوة, كافيه
pub, bar	bār (m)	بار
tearoom	ṣalone ʃāy (m)	صالون شاي
waiter	garsone (m)	جرسون
waitress	garsona (f)	جرسونة
bartender	bārman (m)	بارمان
menu	qā'emet el ṭa'ām (f)	قائمة طعام
wine list	qā'emet el χomūr (f)	قائمة خمور
to book a table	ḥagaz sofra	حجز سفرة
course, dish	wagba (f)	وجبة
to order (meal)	ṭalab	طلب
to make an order	ṭalab	طلب
aperitif	ʃarāb (m)	شراب
appetizer	moqabbelāt (pl)	مقبّلات
dessert	ḥalawīāt (pl)	حلويّات
check	ḥesāb (m)	حساب
to pay the check	dafa' el ḥesāb	دفع الحساب
to give change	edda el bā'y	ادّي الباقي
tip	ba'ʃīʃ (m)	بقشيش

50. Meals

food	akl (m)	أكل
to eat (vi, vt)	akal	أكل
breakfast	foṭūr (m)	فطور
to have breakfast	feṭer	فطر
lunch	ɣada' (m)	غداء
to have lunch	etɣadda	إتغدّى
dinner	'aʃā' (m)	عشاء
to have dinner	et'asʃa	إتعشّى
appetite	ʃahiya (f)	شهيّة
Enjoy your meal!	bel hana wel ʃefa!	!بالهنا والشفا
to open (~ a bottle)	fataḥ	فتح
to spill (liquid)	dala'	دلق
to spill out (vi)	dala'	دلق
to boil (vi)	ɣely	غلى
to boil (vt)	ɣely	غلى
boiled (~ water)	maɣly	مغلي
to chill, cool down (vt)	barrad	برّد
to chill (vi)	barrad	برّد
taste, flavor	ṭa'm (m)	طعم
aftertaste	ṭa'm ma ba'd el mazāq (m)	طعم ما بعد المذاق
to slim down (lose weight)	xass	خسّ
diet	reʒīm (m)	رجيم
vitamin	vitamīn (m)	فيتامين
calorie	so'ra ḥarāriya (f)	سعرة حراريّة
vegetarian (n)	nabāty (m)	نباتي
vegetarian (adj)	nabāty	نباتي
fats (nutrient)	dohūn (pl)	دهون
proteins	brotenāt (pl)	بروتينات
carbohydrates	naʃawīāt (pl)	نشويّات
slice (of lemon, ham)	ʃarīḥa (f)	شريحة
piece (of cake, pie)	'eṭ'a (f)	قطعة
crumb (of bread, cake, etc.)	fattāta (f)	فتاتة

51. Cooked dishes

course, dish	wagba (f)	وجبة
cuisine	maṭbax (m)	مطبخ
recipe	waṣfa (f)	وصفة
portion	naṣīb (m)	نصيب

salad	solṭa (f)	سلطة
soup	ʃorba (f)	شوربة
clear soup (broth)	mara'a (m)	مرقة
sandwich (bread)	sandawitʃ (m)	ساندويتش
fried eggs	beyḍ ma'ly (m)	بيض مقلي
hamburger (beefburger)	hamburger (m)	هامبورجر
beefsteak	steak laḥm (m)	ستيك لحم
side dish	ṭaba' gāneby (m)	طبق جانبي
spaghetti	spaɣetti (m)	سباجيتي
mashed potatoes	baṭāṭes mahrūsa (f)	بطاطس مهروسة
pizza	bītza (f)	بيتزا
porridge (oatmeal, etc.)	'aṣīda (f)	عصيدة
omelet	omlette (m)	اومليت
boiled (e.g., ~ beef)	maslū'	مسلوق
smoked (adj)	modakχen	مدخّن
fried (adj)	ma'ly	مقلي
dried (adj)	mogaffaf	مجفّف
frozen (adj)	mogammad	مجمّد
pickled (adj)	meχallel	مخلّل
sweet (sugary)	mesakkar	مسكّر
salty (adj)	māleḥ	مالح
cold (adj)	bāred	بارد
hot (adj)	soχn	سخن
bitter (adj)	morr	مرّ
tasty (adj)	ḥelw	حلو
to cook in boiling water	sala'	سلق
to cook (dinner)	ḥaḍḍar	حضّر
to fry (vt)	'ala	قلي
to heat up (food)	sakχan	سخّن
to salt (vt)	raʃ malḥ	رشّ ملح
to pepper (vt)	raʃ felfel	رشّ فلفل
to grate (vt)	baraʃ	برش
peel (n)	'eʃra (f)	قشرة
to peel (vt)	'asʃar	قشّر

52. Food

meat	laḥma (f)	لحمة
chicken	ferāχ (m)	فراخ
Rock Cornish hen (poussin)	farrūg (m)	فرّوج
duck	baṭṭa (f)	بطّة
goose	wezza (f)	وزّة

game	ṣeyd (m)	صيد
turkey	dīk rūmy (m)	ديك رومي
pork	laḥm el χanazīr (m)	لحم الخنزير
veal	laḥm el ʻegl (m)	لحم العجل
lamb	laḥm ḍāny (m)	لحم ضاني
beef	laḥm baqary (m)	لحم بقري
rabbit	laḥm arāneb (m)	لحم أرانب
sausage (bologna, pepperoni, etc.)	sogo'' (m)	سجق
vienna sausage (frankfurter)	sogo'' (m)	سجق
bacon	bakon (m)	بيكون
ham	hām(m)	هام
gammon	faχd χanzīr (m)	فخد خنزير
pâté	maʻgūn laḥm (m)	معجون لحم
liver	kebda (f)	كبدة
hamburger (ground beef)	hamburger (m)	هامبورجر
tongue	lesān (m)	لسان
egg	beyḍa (f)	بيضة
eggs	beyḍ (m)	بيض
egg white	bayāḍ el beyḍ (m)	بياض البيض
egg yolk	ṣafār el beyḍ (m)	صفار البيض
fish	samak (m)	سمك
seafood	sīfūd (pl)	سي فود
caviar	kaviar (m)	كافيار
crab	kaboria (m)	كابوريا
shrimp	gammbary (m)	جمبري
oyster	maḥār (m)	محار
spiny lobster	estakoza (m)	استاكوزا
octopus	aχṭabūṭ (m)	أخطبوط
squid	kalmāry (m)	كالماري
sturgeon	samak el ḥafʃ (m)	سمك الحفش
salmon	salamon (m)	سلمون
halibut	samak el halbūt (m)	سمك الهلبوت
cod	samak el qadd (m)	سمك القد
mackerel	makerel (m)	ماكريل
tuna	tuna (f)	تونة
eel	ḥankalīs (m)	حنكليس
trout	salamon mera''aṭ (m)	سلمون مرقّط
sardine	sardīn (m)	سردين
pike	samak el karāky (m)	سمك الكراكي
herring	renga (f)	رنجة
bread	ʻeyʃ (m)	عيش

cheese	gebna (f)	جبنة
sugar	sokkar (m)	سكّر
salt	melḥ (m)	ملح
rice	rozz (m)	رزّ
pasta (macaroni)	makaruna (f)	مكرونة
noodles	nūdles (f)	نودلز
butter	zebda (f)	زبّدة
vegetable oil	zeyt (m)	زيت
sunflower oil	zeyt 'abbād el ʃams (m)	زيت عبّاد الشمس
margarine	margarīn (m)	مارجرين
olives	zaytūn (m)	زيتون
olive oil	zeyt el zaytūn (m)	زيت الزيتون
milk	laban (m)	لبن
condensed milk	ḥalīb mokassaf (m)	حليب مكثّف
yogurt	zabādy (m)	زبادي
sour cream	kreyma ḥamḍa (f)	كريمة حامضة
cream (of milk)	krīma (f)	كريمة
mayonnaise	mayonnɛ:z (m)	مايونيز
buttercream	krīmet zebda (f)	كريمة زبدة
cereal grains (wheat, etc.)	ḥobūb 'amḥ (pl)	حبوب قمح
flour	de'ī' (m)	دقيق
canned food	mo'allabāt (pl)	معلّبات
cornflakes	korn fleks (m)	كورن فليكس
honey	'asal (m)	عسل
jam	mrabba (m)	مربّى
chewing gum	lebān (m)	لبان

53. Drinks

water	meyāh (f)	مياه
drinking water	mayet ʃorb (m)	ميّة شرب
mineral water	maya ma'daniya (f)	ميّة معدنية
still (adj)	rakeda	راكدة
carbonated (adj)	kanz	كانز
sparkling (adj)	kanz	كانز
ice	talg (m)	ثلج
with ice	bel talg	بالتلج
non-alcoholic (adj)	men ɣeyr koḥūl	من غير كحول
soft drink	maʃrūb ɣāzy (m)	مشروب غازي
refreshing drink	ḥāga sa''a (f)	حاجة ساقعة
lemonade	limonāta (f)	ليموناتة

liquors	maʃrūbāt koḥūliya (pl)	مشروبات كحولية
wine	χamra (f)	خمرة
white wine	nebīz abyaḍ (m)	نبيذ أبيض
red wine	nebī aḥmar (m)	نبيذ أحمر
liqueur	liqure (m)	ليكيور
champagne	ʃambania (f)	شمبانيا
vermouth	vermote (m)	فيرموت
whiskey	wiski (m)	ويسكي
vodka	vodka (f)	فودكا
gin	ʒin (m)	جين
cognac	konyāk (m)	كونياك
rum	rum (m)	رم
coffee	'ahwa (f)	قهوة
black coffee	'ahwa sāda (f)	قهوة سادة
coffee with milk	'ahwa bel ḥalīb (f)	قهوة بالحليب
cappuccino	kaputʃino (m)	كابتشينو
instant coffee	neskafe (m)	نيسكافيه
milk	laban (m)	لبن
cocktail	koktayl (m)	كوكتيل
milkshake	milk ʃejk (m)	ميلك شيك
juice	ʿaṣīr (m)	عصير
tomato juice	ʿaṣīr ṭamāṭem (m)	عصير طماطم
orange juice	ʿaṣīr bortoqāl (m)	عصير برتقال
freshly squeezed juice	ʿaṣīr freʃ (m)	عصير فريش
beer	bīra (f)	بيرة
light beer	bīra χafīfa (f)	بيرة خفيفة
dark beer	bīra ɣam'a (f)	بيرة غامقة
tea	ʃāy (m)	شاي
black tea	ʃāy aḥmar (m)	شاي أحمر
green tea	ʃāy aχḍar (m)	شاي أخضر

54. Vegetables

vegetables	χoḍār (pl)	خضار
greens	χoḍrawāt waraqiya (pl)	خضروات ورقية
tomato	ṭamāṭem (f)	طماطم
cucumber	χeyār (m)	خيار
carrot	gazar (m)	جزر
potato	baṭāṭes (f)	بطاطس
onion	baṣal (m)	بصل
garlic	tūm (m)	ثوم
cabbage	koronb (m)	كرنب

cauliflower	'arnabīṭ (m)	قرنبيط
Brussels sprouts	koronb broksel (m)	كرنب بروكسل
broccoli	brokkoli (m)	بركولي
beetroot	bangar (m)	بنجر
eggplant	bātengān (m)	باذنجان
zucchini	kōsa (f)	كوسة
pumpkin	qar' 'asaly (m)	قرع عسلي
turnip	left (m)	لفت
parsley	ba'dūnes (m)	بقدونس
dill	ʃabat (m)	شبت
lettuce	χass (m)	خسّ
celery	karfas (m)	كرفس
asparagus	helione (m)	هليون
spinach	sabāneχ (m)	سبانخ
pea	besella (f)	بسلّة
beans	fūl (m)	فول
corn (maize)	dora (f)	ذرة
kidney bean	faṣolya (f)	فاصوليا
bell pepper	felfel (m)	فلفل
radish	fegl (m)	فجل
artichoke	χarʃūf (m)	خرشوف

55. Fruits. Nuts

fruit	faχa (f)	فاكهة
apple	toffāḥa (f)	تفّاحة
pear	komettra (f)	كمّثرى
lemon	lymūn (m)	ليمون
orange	bortoqāl (m)	برتقال
strawberry (garden ~)	farawla (f)	فراولة
mandarin	yosfy (m)	يوسفي
plum	bar'ū' (m)	برقوق
peach	χawχa (f)	خوخة
apricot	meʃmeʃ (f)	مشمش
raspberry	tūt el 'alī' el aḥmar (m)	توت العليق الأحمر
pineapple	ananās (m)	أناناس
banana	moze (m)	موز
watermelon	baṭṭīχ (m)	بطّيخ
grape	'enab (m)	عنب
cherry	karaz (m)	كرز
melon	ʃammām (f)	شمّام
grapefruit	grabe frūt (m)	جريب فروت
avocado	avokado (f)	افوكاتو

papaya	babāya (m)	ببايا
mango	manga (m)	مانجة
pomegranate	rommān (m)	رمان
redcurrant	keʃmeʃ aḥmar (m)	كشمش أحمر
blackcurrant	keʃmeʃ aswad (m)	كشمش أسود
gooseberry	'enab el sa'lab (m)	عنب الثعلب
bilberry	'enab al aḥrāg (m)	عنب الأحراج
blackberry	tūt aswad (m)	توت أسود
raisin	zebīb (m)	زبيب
fig	tīn (m)	تين
date	tamr (m)	تمر
peanut	fūl sudāny (m)	فول سوداني
almond	loze (m)	لوز
walnut	'eyn gamal (f)	عين الجمل
hazelnut	bondo' (m)	بندق
coconut	goze el hend (m)	جوز هند
pistachios	fosto' (m)	فستق

56. Bread. Candy

bakers' confectionery (pastry)	ḥalawīāt (pl)	حلويّات
bread	'eyʃ (m)	عيش
cookies	baskawīt (m)	بسكويت
chocolate (n)	ʃokolāta (f)	شكولاتة
chocolate (as adj)	bel ʃokolāṭa	بالشكولاتة
candy (wrapped)	bonbony (m)	بونبوني
cake (e.g., cupcake)	keyka (f)	كيكة
cake (e.g., birthday ~)	torta (f)	تورتة
pie (e.g., apple ~)	feṭīra (f)	فطيرة
filling (for cake, pie)	ḥaʃwa (f)	حشوة
jam (whole fruit jam)	mrabba (m)	مربّى
marmalade	marmalād (f)	مرملاد
waffles	waffles (pl)	وافلز
ice-cream	'ays krīm (m)	آيس كريم
pudding	būding (m)	بودنج

57. Spices

salt	melḥ (m)	ملح
salty (adj)	māleḥ	مالِح
to salt (vt)	rasʃ malḥ	رش ملح

black pepper	felfel aswad (m)	فلفل أسوّد
red pepper (milled ~)	felfel aḥmar (m)	فلفل أحمر
mustard	mosṭarda (m)	مسطردة
horseradish	fegl ḥār (m)	فجل حار
condiment	bahār (m)	بهار
spice	bahār (m)	بهار
sauce	ṣalṣa (f)	صلصة
vinegar	χall (m)	خلّ
anise	yansūn (m)	ينسون
basil	rīḥān (m)	ريحان
cloves	ʾoronfol (m)	قرنفل
ginger	zangabīl (m)	زنجبيل
coriander	kozbora (f)	كزبرة
cinnamon	ʾerfa (f)	قرفة
sesame	semsem (m)	سمسم
bay leaf	waraʾ el ɣār (m)	ورق الغار
paprika	babrika (f)	بابريكا
caraway	karawya (f)	كراوية
saffron	zaʿfarān (m)	زعفران

PERSONAL INFORMATION. FAMILY

58. Personal information. Forms

name (first name)	esm (m)	اسم
surname (last name)	esm el 'a'ela (m)	اسم العائلة
date of birth	tarīχ el melād (m)	تاريخ الميلاد
place of birth	makān el melād (m)	مكان الميلاد
nationality	gensiya (f)	جنسيّة
place of residence	maqarr el eqāma (m)	مقرّ الإقامة
country	balad (m)	بلد
profession (occupation)	mehna (f)	مهنة
gender, sex	ginss (m)	جنس
height	ṭūl (m)	طول
weight	wazn (m)	وزن

59. Family members. Relatives

mother	walda (f)	والدة
father	wāled (m)	والد
son	walad (m)	ولد
daughter	bent (f)	بنت
younger daughter	el bent el saɣīra (f)	البنت الصغيرة
younger son	el ebn el saɣīr (m)	الابن الصغير
eldest daughter	el bent el kebīra (f)	البنت الكبيرة
eldest son	el ebn el kabīr (m)	الابن الكبير
brother	aχ (m)	أخ
elder brother	el aχ el kibīr (m)	الأخ الكبير
younger brother	el aχ el ṣoɣeyyir (m)	الأخ الصغير
sister	oχt (f)	أخت
elder sister	el uχt el kibīra (f)	الأخت الكبيرة
younger sister	el uχt el ṣoɣeyyira (f)	الأخت الصغيرة
cousin (masc.)	ibn 'amm (m), ibn χāl (m)	إبن عمّ, إبن خال
cousin (fem.)	bint 'amm (f), bint χāl (f)	بنت عمّ, بنت خال
mom, mommy	mama (f)	ماما
dad, daddy	baba (m)	بابا
parents	waldeyn (du)	والدين
child	ṭefl (m)	طفل
children	aṭfāl (pl)	أطفال

grandmother	gedda (f)	جدّة
grandfather	gadd (m)	جدّ
grandson	ḥafīd (m)	حفيد
granddaughter	ḥafīda (f)	حفيدة
grandchildren	aḥfād (pl)	أحفاد
uncle	ʿamm (m), χāl (m)	عمّ, خال
aunt	ʿamma (f), χāla (f)	عمّة, خالة
nephew	ibn el aχ (m), ibn el uχt (m)	إبن الأخ, إبن الأخت
niece	bint el aχ (f), bint el uχt (f)	بنت الأخ, بنت الأخت
mother-in-law (wife's mother)	ḥamah (f)	حماة
father-in-law (husband's father)	ḥama (m)	حما
son-in-law (daughter's husband)	goze el bent (m)	جوز البنت
stepmother	merāt el abb (f)	مرات الأب
stepfather	goze el omm (m)	جوز الأم
infant	ṭefl raḍeeʿ (m)	طفل رضيع
baby (infant)	mawlūd (m)	موّلود
little boy, kid	walad ṣaɣīr (m)	ولد صغير
wife	goza (f)	جوزة
husband	goze (m)	جوز
spouse (husband)	goze (m)	جوز
spouse (wife)	goza (f)	جوزة
married (masc.)	metgawwez	متجوّز
married (fem.)	metgawweza	متجوّزة
single (unmarried)	aʿzab	أعزب
bachelor	aʿzab (m)	أعزب
divorced (masc.)	moṭallaq (m)	مطلّق
widow	armala (f)	أرملة
widower	armal (m)	أرمل
relative	ʾarīb (m)	قريب
close relative	nesīb ʾarīb (m)	نسيب قريب
distant relative	nesīb beʿīd (m)	نسيب بعيد
relatives	aqāreb (pl)	أقارب
orphan (boy or girl)	yatīm (m)	يتيم
guardian (of a minor)	walyī amr (m)	وليّ أمر
to adopt (a boy)	tabanna	تبنّى
to adopt (a girl)	tabanna	تبنّى

60. Friends. Coworkers

friend (masc.)	ṣadīq (m)	صديق
friend (fem.)	ṣadīqa (f)	صديقة

friendship	ṣadāqa (f)	صداقة
to be friends	ṣādaq	صادق
buddy (masc.)	ṣāḥeb (m)	صاحب
buddy (fem.)	ṣaḥba (f)	صاحبة
partner	rafī' (m)	رفيق
chief (boss)	ra'īs (m)	رئيس
superior (n)	el arfa' maqāman (m)	الأرفع مقاماً
owner, proprietor	ṣāḥib (m)	صاحب
subordinate (n)	tābe' (m)	تابع
colleague	zamīl (m)	زميل
acquaintance (person)	ma'refa (m)	معرفة
fellow traveler	rafī' safar (m)	رفيق سفر
classmate	zamīl fel ṣaff (m)	زميل في الصفّ
neighbor (masc.)	gār (m)	جار
neighbor (fem.)	gāra (f)	جارة
neighbors	gerān (pl)	جيران

HUMAN BODY. MEDICINE

61. Head

head	ra'ʾs (m)	رأس
face	weʃ (m)	وش
nose	manaχīr (m)	مناخير
mouth	bo' (m)	بوء
eye	'eyn (f)	عين
eyes	'oyūn (pl)	عيون
pupil	ḥad'a (f)	حدقة
eyebrow	ḥāgeb (m)	حاجب
eyelash	remʃ (m)	رمش
eyelid	gefn (m)	جفن
tongue	lesān (m)	لسان
tooth	senna (f)	سنّة
lips	ʃafāyef (pl)	شفايف
cheekbones	'aḍmet el χadd (f)	عضمة الخدّ
gum	lassa (f)	لثّة
palate	ḥanak (m)	حنك
nostrils	manaχer (pl)	مناخر
chin	da''n (m)	دقن
jaw	fakk (m)	فكّ
cheek	χadd (m)	خدّ
forehead	gabha (f)	جبهة
temple	ṣedɣ (m)	صدغ
ear	wedn (f)	ودن
back of the head	'afa (m)	قفا
neck	ra'aba (f)	رقبة
throat	zore (m)	زور
hair	ʃa'r (m)	شعر
hairstyle	tasrīḥa (f)	تسريحة
haircut	tasrīḥa (f)	تسريحة
wig	barūka (f)	باروكة
mustache	ʃanab (pl)	شنب
beard	leḥya (f)	لحية
to have (a beard, etc.)	'ando	عنده
braid	ḍefīra (f)	ضفيرة
sideburns	sawālef (pl)	سوالف
red-haired (adj)	aḥmar el ʃa'r	أحمر الشعر

gray (hair)	ʃaʿr abyaḍ	شعر أبيض
bald (adj)	aṣlaʿ	أصلع
bald patch	ṣalaʿ (m)	صلع
ponytail	deyl ḥoṣān (m)	ديل حصان
bangs	ʾoṣṣa (f)	قصّة

62. Human body

hand	yad (m)	يد
arm	derāʿ (f)	دراع
finger	ṣobāʿ (m)	صباع
toe	ṣobāʿ el ʾadam (m)	صباع القدم
thumb	ebhām (m)	إبهام
little finger	χonṣor (m)	خنصر
nail	ḍefr (m)	ضفر
fist	qabḍa (f)	قبضة
palm	kaff (f)	كفّ
wrist	meʿṣam (m)	معصم
forearm	sāʿed (m)	ساعد
elbow	kūʿ (m)	كوع
shoulder	ketf (f)	كتف
leg	regl (f)	رجل
foot	qadam (f)	قدم
knee	rokba (f)	ركبة
calf (part of leg)	semmāna (f)	سمّانة
hip	faχd (f)	فخد
heel	kaʿb (m)	كعب
body	gesm (m)	جسم
stomach	baṭn (m)	بطن
chest	ṣedr (m)	صدر
breast	sady (m)	ثدي
flank	ganb (m)	جنب
back	ḍahr (m)	ضهر
lower back	asfal el ḍahr (m)	أسفل الضهر
waist	wesṭ (f)	وسط
navel (belly button)	sorra (f)	سرّة
buttocks	ardāf (pl)	أرداف
bottom	debr (m)	دبر
beauty mark	ʃāma (f)	شامة
birthmark (café au lait spot)	waḥma	وحمة
tattoo	waʃm (m)	وشم
scar	nadba (f)	ندبة

63. Diseases

sickness	maraḍ (m)	مرض
to be sick	mereḍ	مرض
health	ṣeḥḥa (f)	صحّة
runny nose (coryza)	raʃ-ḥ fel anf (m)	رشح في الأنف
tonsillitis	eltehāb el lawzateyn (m)	إلتهاب اللوزتين
cold (illness)	zokām (m)	زكام
to catch a cold	gālo bard	جاله برد
bronchitis	eltehāb ʃo'aby (m)	إلتهاب شعبيّ
pneumonia	eltehāb ra'awy (m)	إلتهاب رئوي
flu, influenza	influenza (f)	إنفلونزا
nearsighted (adj)	'aṣīr el naẓar	قصير النظر
farsighted (adj)	be'īd el naẓar	بعيد النظر
strabismus (crossed eyes)	ḥawal (m)	حوّل
cross-eyed (adj)	aḥwal	أحوّل
cataract	katarakt (f)	كاتاراكت
glaucoma	glawkoma (f)	جلوكوما
stroke	sakta (f)	سكتة
heart attack	azma 'albiya (f)	أزمة قلبية
myocardial infarction	nawba 'albiya (f)	نوبة قلبية
paralysis	ʃalal (m)	شلل
to paralyze (vt)	ʃall	شلّ
allergy	ḥasasiya (f)	حساسيّة
asthma	rabw (m)	ربو
diabetes	dā' el sokkary (m)	داء السكّري
toothache	alam asnān (m)	ألم الأسنان
caries	naχr el asnān (m)	نخر الأسنان
diarrhea	es-hāl (m)	إسهال
constipation	emsāk (m)	إمساك
stomach upset	edṭrāb el me'da (m)	إضطراب المعدة
food poisoning	tasammom (m)	تسمم
to get food poisoning	etsammem	إتسمّم
arthritis	eltehāb el mafāṣel (m)	إلتهاب المفاصل
rickets	kosāḥ el aṭfāl (m)	كساح الأطفال
rheumatism	rheumatism (m)	روماتزم
atherosclerosis	taṣṣallob el ʃarayīn (m)	تصلّب الشرايين
gastritis	eltehāb el me'da (m)	إلتهاب المعدة
appendicitis	eltehāb el zayda el dūdiya (m)	إلتهاب الزائدة الدودية
cholecystitis	eltehāb el marāra (m)	إلتهاب المرارة
ulcer	qorḥa (f)	قرحة

measles	maraḍ el ḥaṣba (m)	مرض الحصبة
rubella (German measles)	el ḥaṣba el almaniya (f)	الحصبة الألمانية
jaundice	yaraqān (m)	يرقان
hepatitis	eltehāb el kabed el vayrūsy (m)	إلتهاب الكبد الفيروسي
schizophrenia	fuṣām (m)	فصام
rabies (hydrophobia)	dā' el kalb (m)	داء الكلب
neurosis	eḍṭrāb 'aṣaby (m)	إضطراب عصبي
concussion	ertegāg el moχ (m)	إرتجاج المخ
cancer	saraṭān (m)	سرطان
sclerosis	taṣṣallob (m)	تصلّب
multiple sclerosis	taṣṣallob mota'added (m)	تصلّب متعدّد
alcoholism	edmān el χamr (m)	إدمان الخمر
alcoholic (n)	modmen el χamr (m)	مدمن الخمر
syphilis	syfilis el zehry (m)	سفلس الزهري
AIDS	el eydz (m)	الايدز
tumor	waram (m)	ورم
malignant (adj)	χabīs	خبيث
benign (adj)	ḥamīd (m)	حميد
fever	ḥomma (f)	حمّى
malaria	malaria (f)	ملاريا
gangrene	ɣanɣarīna (f)	غنغرينا
seasickness	dawār el baḥr (m)	دوار البحر
epilepsy	maraḍ el ṣara' (m)	مرض الصرع
epidemic	wabā' (m)	وباء
typhus	tyfus (m)	تيفوس
tuberculosis	maraḍ el soll (m)	مرض السلّ
cholera	kōlīra (f)	كوليرا
plague (bubonic ~)	ṭa'ūn (m)	طاعون

64. Symptoms. Treatments. Part 1

symptom	'araḍ (m)	عرض
temperature	ḥarāra (f)	حرارة
high temperature (fever)	ḥomma (f)	حمّى
pulse	nabḍ (m)	نبض
dizziness (vertigo)	dawχa (f)	دوخة
hot (adj)	soχn	سخن
shivering	ra'ʃa (f)	رعشة
pale (e.g., ~ face)	aṣfar	أصفر
cough	koḥḥa (f)	كحّة
to cough (vi)	kaḥḥ	كحّ
to sneeze (vi)	'aṭas	عطس

faint	dawχa (f)	دوخة
to faint (vi)	oɣma ʿaleyh	أغمي عليه
bruise (hématome)	kadma (f)	كدمة
bump (lump)	tawarrom (m)	تورّم
to bang (bump)	etχabaṭ	إتخبط
contusion (bruise)	raḍḍa (f)	رضّة
to get a bruise	etkadam	إتكدم
to limp (vi)	ʿarag	عرج
dislocation	χalʿ (m)	خلع
to dislocate (vt)	χalaʿ	خلع
fracture	kasr (m)	كسر
to have a fracture	enkasar	إنكسر
cut (e.g., paper ~)	garḥ (m)	جرح
to cut oneself	garaḥ nafsoh	جرح نفسه
bleeding	nazīf (m)	نزيف
burn (injury)	ḥarʾ (m)	حرق
to get burned	et-ḥaraʾ	إتحرق
to prick (vt)	waχaz	وخز
to prick oneself	waχaz nafso	وخز نفسه
to injure (vt)	aṣāb	أصاب
injury	eṣāba (f)	إصابة
wound	garḥ (m)	جرح
trauma	ṣadma (f)	صدمة
to be delirious	haza	هذى
to stutter (vi)	talaʿsam	تلعثم
sunstroke	ḍarabet ʃams (f)	ضربة شمس

65. Symptoms. Treatments. Part 2

pain, ache	alam (m)	ألم
splinter (in foot, etc.)	ʃazya (f)	شظية
sweat (perspiration)	ʿerʾ (m)	عرق
to sweat (perspire)	ʿereʾ	عرق
vomiting	targeeʿ (m)	ترجيع
convulsions	taʃonnogāt (pl)	تشنّجات
pregnant (adj)	ḥāmel	حامل
to be born	etwalad	اتّولد
delivery, labor	welāda (f)	ولادة
to deliver (~ a baby)	walad	ولد
abortion	eg-hāḍ (m)	إجهاض
breathing, respiration	tanaffos (m)	تنفّس
in-breath (inhalation)	estenʃāq (m)	إستنشاق

out-breath (exhalation)	zafīr (m)	زفير
to exhale (breathe out)	zafar	زفر
to inhale (vi)	estanʃaq	إستنشق
disabled person	mo'āq (m)	معاق
cripple	moq'ad (m)	مقعد
drug addict	modmen moχaddarāt (m)	مدمن مخدّرات
deaf (adj)	aṭraʃ	أطرش
mute (adj)	aχras	أخرس
deaf mute (adj)	aṭraʃ aχras	أطرش أخرس
mad, insane (adj)	magnūn (m)	مجنون
madman (demented person)	magnūn (m)	مجنون
madwoman	magnūna (f)	مجنونة
to go insane	etgannen	اتجنّن
gene	ʒīn (m)	جين
immunity	manā'a (f)	مناعة
hereditary (adj)	werāsy	وراثي
congenital (adj)	χolqy men el welāda	خلقي من الولادة
virus	virūs (m)	فيروس
microbe	mikrūb (m)	ميكروب
bacterium	garsūma (f)	جرثومة
infection	'adwa (f)	عدوى

66. Symptoms. Treatments. Part 3

hospital	mostaʃfa (m)	مستشفى
patient	marīḍ (m)	مريض
diagnosis	taʃχīṣ (m)	تشخيص
cure	ʃefā' (m)	شفاء
medical treatment	'elāg ṭebby (m)	علاج طبي
to get treatment	et'āleg	اتعالج
to treat (~ a patient)	'ālag	عالج
to nurse (look after)	marraḍ	مرّض
care (nursing ~)	'enāya (f)	عناية
operation, surgery	'amaliya grāḥiya (f)	عمليّة جراحية
to bandage (head, limb)	ḍammad	ضمّد
bandaging	taḍmīd (m)	تضميد
vaccination	talqīḥ (m)	تلقيح
to vaccinate (vt)	laqqaḥ	لقّح
injection, shot	ḥo'na (f)	حقنة
to give an injection	ḥa'an ebra	حقن إبرة
attack	nawba (f)	نوبة

amputation	batr (m)	بتر
to amputate (vt)	batr	بتر
coma	ɣaybūba (f)	غيبوبة
to be in a coma	kān fi ḥālet ɣaybūba	كان في حالة غيبوبة
intensive care	el ʻenāya el morakkaza (f)	العناية المركّزة
to recover (~ from flu)	ʃefy	شفي
condition (patient's ~)	ḥāla (f)	حالة
consciousness	wa'y (m)	وعي
memory (faculty)	zākera (f)	ذاكرة
to pull out (tooth)	χala'	خلع
filling	ḥaʃww (m)	حشو
to fill (a tooth)	ḥaʃa	حشا
hypnosis	el tanwīm el meɣnaṭīsy (m)	التنويم المغناطيسي
to hypnotize (vt)	nawwem	نوّم

67. Medicine. Drugs. Accessories

medicine, drug	dawā' (m)	دواء
remedy	ʻelāg (m)	علاج
to prescribe (vt)	waṣaf	وصف
prescription	waṣfa (f)	وصفة
tablet, pill	'orṣ (m)	قرص
ointment	marham (m)	مرهم
ampule	ambūla (f)	أمبولة
mixture	dawā' ʃorb (m)	دواء شراب
syrup	ʃarāb (m)	شراب
pill	ḥabba (f)	حبّة
powder	zorūr (m)	ذرور
gauze bandage	ḍammāda ʃāʃ (f)	ضمادة شاش
cotton wool	'oṭn (m)	قطن
iodine	yūd (m)	يود
Band-Aid	blaster (m)	بلاستر
eyedropper	'aṭṭāra (f)	قطّارة
thermometer	termometr (m)	ترمومتر
syringe	serennga (f)	سرنّجة
wheelchair	korsy motaḥarrek (m)	كرسي متحرك
crutches	ʻokkāz (m)	عكّاز
painkiller	mosakken (m)	مسكّن
laxative	molayen (m)	مليّن
spirits (ethanol)	etanol (m)	إيثانول
medicinal herbs	aʻʃāb ṭebbiya (pl)	أعشاب طبيّة
herbal (~ tea)	ʻoʃby	عشبي

APARTMENT

68. Apartment

apartment	ʃa''a (f)	شقّة
room	oḍa (f)	أوضة
bedroom	oḍet el nome (f)	أوضة النوم
dining room	oḍet el sofra (f)	أوضة السفرة
living room	oḍet el esteqbāl (f)	أوضة الإستقبال
study (home office)	maktab (m)	مكتب
entry room	madχal (m)	مدخل
bathroom (room with a bath or shower)	ḥammām (m)	حمّام
half bath	ḥammām (m)	حمّام
ceiling	sa'f (m)	سقف
floor	arḍiya (f)	أرضية
corner	zawya (f)	زاوية

69. Furniture. Interior

furniture	asās (m)	أثاث
table	maktab (m)	مكتب
chair	korsy (m)	كرسي
bed	serīr (m)	سرير
couch, sofa	kanaba (f)	كنبة
armchair	korsy (m)	كرسي
bookcase	χazzānet kotob (f)	خزّانة كتب
shelf	raff (m)	رفّ
wardrobe	dolāb (m)	دولاب
coat rack (wall-mounted ~)	ʃammāʿa (f)	شمّاعة
coat stand	ʃammāʿa (f)	شمّاعة
bureau, dresser	dolāb adrāg (m)	دولاب أدراج
coffee table	ṭarabeyzet el 'ahwa (f)	طرابيزة القهوة
mirror	merāya (f)	مراية
carpet	seggāda (f)	سجّادة
rug, small carpet	seggāda (f)	سجّادة
fireplace	daffāya (f)	دفّاية
candle	ʃamʿa (f)	شمعة

candlestick	ʃamʿadān (m)	شمعدان
drapes	satā'er (pl)	ستائر
wallpaper	wara' ḥā'eṭ (m)	ورق حائط
blinds (jalousie)	satā'er ofoqiya (pl)	ستائر أفقيّة
table lamp	abāʒūr (f)	اباجورة
wall lamp (sconce)	lammbet ḥā'eṭ (f)	لمّبة حائط
floor lamp	meṣbāḥ arḍy (m)	مصباح أرضي
chandelier	nagafa (f)	نجفة
leg (of chair, table)	regl (f)	رجل
armrest	masnad (m)	مسند
back (backrest)	masnad (m)	مسند
drawer	dorg (m)	درج

70. Bedding

bedclothes	bayāḍāt el serīr (pl)	بياضات السرير
pillow	maχadda (f)	مخدّة
pillowcase	kīs el maχadda (m)	كيس المخدّة
duvet, comforter	leḥāf (m)	لحاف
sheet	melāya (f)	ملاية
bedspread	ɣaṭā' el serīr (m)	غطاء السرير

71. Kitchen

kitchen	maṭbaχ (m)	مطبخ
gas	ɣāz (m)	غاز
gas stove (range)	botoɣāz (m)	بوتوغاز
electric stove	forn kaharabā'y (m)	فرن كهربائي
oven	forn (m)	فرن
microwave oven	mikroweyv (m)	ميكروويف
refrigerator	tallāga (f)	ثلاجة
freezer	freyzer (m)	فريزر
dishwasher	ɣassālet aṭbā' (f)	غسّالة أطباق
meat grinder	farrāmet laḥm (f)	فرّامة لحم
juicer	ʿaṣṣāra (f)	عصّارة
toaster	maḥmaṣet χobz (f)	محمصة خبز
mixer	χallāṭ (m)	خلّاط
coffee machine	makinet ṣonʿ el 'ahwa (f)	ماكينة صنع القهوة
coffee pot	ɣallāya kahraba'iya (f)	غلّاية القهوة
coffee grinder	maṭ-ḥanet 'ahwa (f)	مطحنة قهوة
kettle	ɣallāya (f)	غلّاية
teapot	barrād el ʃāy (m)	برّاد الشاي

lid	ɣaṭā' (m)	غطاء
tea strainer	maṣfāh el ʃāy (f)	مصفاة الشاي
spoon	ma'la'a (f)	معلقة
teaspoon	ma'la'et ʃāy (f)	معلقة شاي
soup spoon	ma'la'a kebīra (f)	ملعقة كبيرة
fork	ʃawka (f)	شوكة
knife	sekkīna (f)	سكّينة
tableware (dishes)	awāny (pl)	أواني
plate (dinner ~)	ṭaba' (m)	طبق
saucer	ṭaba' fengān (m)	طبق فنجان
shot glass	kāsa (f)	كاسة
glass (tumbler)	kobbāya (f)	كوبّاية
cup	fengān (m)	فنجان
sugar bowl	sokkariya (f)	سكّريّة
salt shaker	mamlaḥa (f)	مملحة
pepper shaker	mobhera (f)	مبهرة
butter dish	ṭaba' zebda (m)	طبق زبدة
stock pot (soup pot)	ḥalla (f)	حلّة
frying pan (skillet)	ṭāsa (f)	طاسة
ladle	maɣrafa (f)	مغرفة
colander	maṣfāh (f)	مصفاه
tray (serving ~)	ṣeniya (f)	صينيّة
bottle	ezāza (f)	إزازة
jar (glass)	barṭamān (m)	برطمان
can	kanz (m)	كانز
bottle opener	fattāḥa (f)	فتّاحة
can opener	fattāḥa (f)	فتّاحة
corkscrew	barrīma (f)	بريّمة
filter	filter (m)	فلتر
to filter (vt)	ṣaffa	صفّى
trash, garbage (food waste, etc.)	zebāla (f)	زبالة
trash can (kitchen ~)	ṣandū' el zebāla (m)	صندوق الزبالة

72. Bathroom

bathroom	ḥammām (m)	حمّام
water	meyāh (f)	مياه
faucet	ḥanafiya (f)	حنفيّة
hot water	maya soχna (f)	مايّة سخنة
cold water	maya barda (f)	مايّة باردة
toothpaste	ma'gūn asnān (m)	معجون أسنان

to brush one's teeth	naḍḍaf el asnān	نظّف الأسنان
toothbrush	forʃet senān (f)	فرشة أسنان
to shave (vi)	ḥala'	حلق
shaving foam	raɣwa lel ḥelā'a (f)	رغوة للحلاقة
razor	mūs (m)	موس
to wash (one's hands, etc.)	ɣasal	غسل
to take a bath	estaḥamma	إستحمّى
shower	doʃ (m)	دوش
to take a shower	aχad doʃ	أخد دوش
bathtub	banyo (m)	بانيو
toilet (toilet bowl)	twalet (m)	تواليت
sink (washbasin)	ḥoḍe (m)	حوض
soap	ṣabūn (m)	صابون
soap dish	ṣabbāna (f)	صبّانة
sponge	līfa (f)	ليفة
shampoo	ʃambū (m)	شامبو
towel	fūṭa (f)	فوطة
bathrobe	robe el ḥammām (m)	روب حمّام
laundry (process)	ɣasīl (m)	غسيل
washing machine	ɣassāla (f)	غسّالة
to do the laundry	ɣasal el malābes	غسل الملابس
laundry detergent	mas-ḥū' ɣasīl (m)	مسحوق غسيل

73. Household appliances

TV set	televizion (m)	تليفزيون
tape recorder	gehāz tasgīl (m)	جهاز تسجيل
VCR (video recorder)	'āla tasgīl video (f)	آلة تسجيل فيديو
radio	gehāz radio (m)	جهاز راديو
player (CD, MP3, etc.)	blayer (m)	بليير
video projector	gehāz 'arḍ (m)	جهاز عرض
home movie theater	sinema manzeliya (f)	سينما منزليّة
DVD player	dividī blayer (m)	دي في دي بليير
amplifier	mokabbaer el ṣote (m)	مكبّر الصوت
video game console	'ātāry (m)	أتاري
video camera	kamera video (f)	كاميرا فيديو
camera (photo)	kamera (f)	كاميرا
digital camera	kamera diʒital (f)	كاميرا ديجيتال
vacuum cleaner	maknasa kahraba'iya (f)	مكنسة كهربائيّة
iron (e.g., steam ~)	makwa (f)	مكواة
ironing board	lawḥet kayī (f)	لوحة كيّ

telephone	telefon (m)	تليفون
cell phone	mobile (m)	موبايل
typewriter	'āla katba (f)	آلة كاتبة
sewing machine	makanet el χeyāṭa (f)	مكنة الخياطة
microphone	mikrofon (m)	ميكروفون
headphones	samma'āt ra'siya (pl)	سمّاعات رأسية
remote control (TV)	remowt kontrol (m)	ريموت كنترول
CD, compact disc	sidī (m)	سي دي
cassette, tape	kasett (m)	كاسيت
vinyl record	esṭewāna mūsīqa (f)	أسطوانة موسيقى

THE EARTH. WEATHER

74. Outer space

space	faḍā' (m)	فضاء
space (as adj)	faḍā'y	فضائي
outer space	el faḍā' el χāregy (m)	الفضاء الخارجي
world	'ālam (m)	عالم
universe	el kōn (m)	الكون
galaxy	el magarra (f)	المجرّة
star	negm (m)	نجم
constellation	borg (m)	برج
planet	kawwkab (m)	كوكب
satellite	'amar ṣenā'y (m)	قمر صناعي
meteorite	nayzek (m)	نيّزك
comet	mozannab (m)	مذنّب
asteroid	kowaykeb (m)	كويكب
orbit	madār (m)	مدار
to revolve (~ around the Earth)	dār	دار
atmosphere	el ɣelāf el gawwy (m)	الغلاف الجوّي
the Sun	el ʃams (f)	الشمس
solar system	el magmū'a el ʃamsiya (f)	المجموعة الشمسيّة
solar eclipse	kosūf el ʃams (m)	كسوف الشمس
the Earth	el arḍ (f)	الأرض
the Moon	el 'amar (m)	القمر
Mars	el marrīχ (m)	المرّيخ
Venus	el zahra (f)	الزهرة
Jupiter	el moʃtary (m)	المشتري
Saturn	zoḥḥol (m)	زحل
Mercury	'aṭāred (m)	عطارد
Uranus	uranus (m)	اورانوس
Neptune	nibtūn (m)	نبتون
Pluto	bluto (m)	بلوتو
Milky Way	darb el tebbāna (m)	درب التبّانة
Great Bear (Ursa Major)	el dobb el akbar (m)	الدب الأكبر
North Star	negm el 'oṭb (m)	نجم القطب
Martian	sāken el marrīχ (m)	ساكن المرّيخ

extraterrestrial (n)	faḍā'y (m)	فضائي
alien	kā'en faḍā'y (m)	كائن فضائي
flying saucer	ṭaba' ṭā'er (m)	طبق طائر
spaceship	markaba faḍa'iya (f)	مركبة فضائية
space station	maḥaṭṭet faḍā' (f)	محطّة فضاء
blast-off	enṭelāq (m)	إنطلاق
engine	motore (m)	موتور
nozzle	manfaθ (m)	منفث
fuel	woqūd (m)	وقود
cockpit, flight deck	kabīna (f)	كابينة
antenna	hawā'y (m)	هوائي
porthole	kowwa mostadīra (f)	كوّة مستديرة
solar panel	lawḥa ʃamsiya (f)	لوحة شمسيّة
spacesuit	badlet el faḍā' (f)	بدّلة الفضاء
weightlessness	en'edām wazn (m)	إنعدام الوزن
oxygen	oksiʒīn (m)	أوكسجين
docking (in space)	rasw (m)	رسو
to dock (vi, vt)	rasa	رسى
observatory	marṣad (m)	مرصد
telescope	teleskop (m)	تلسكوب
to observe (vt)	rāqab	راقب
to explore (vt)	estakʃef	إستكشف

75. The Earth

the Earth	el arḍ (f)	الأرض
the globe (the Earth)	el kora el arḍiya (f)	الكرة الأرضيّة
planet	kawwkab (m)	كوّكب
atmosphere	el ɣelāf el gawwy (m)	الغلاف الجوّي
geography	goɣrafia (f)	جغرافيا
nature	ṭabee'a (f)	طبيعة
globe (table ~)	namūzag lel kora el arḍiya (m)	نموذج للكرة الأرضيّة
map	xarīṭa (f)	خريطة
atlas	aṭlas (m)	أطلس
Europe	orobba (f)	أوروبّا
Asia	asya (f)	آسيا
Africa	afreqia (f)	أفريقيا
Australia	ostorālya (f)	أستراليا
America	amrīka (f)	أمريكا
North America	amrīka el ʃamaliya (f)	أمريكا الشماليّة

South America	amrīka el ganūbiya (f)	أمريكا الجنوبيّة
Antarctica	el qoṭb el ganūby (m)	القطب الجنوبي
the Arctic	el qoṭb el ʃamāly (m)	القطب الشمالي

76. Cardinal directions

north	ʃemāl (m)	شمال
to the north	lel ʃamāl	للشمال
in the north	fel ʃamāl	في الشمال
northern (adj)	ʃamāly	شمالي
south	ganūb (m)	جنوب
to the south	lel ganūb	للجنوب
in the south	fel ganūb	في الجنوب
southern (adj)	ganūby	جنوبي
west	ɣarb (m)	غرب
to the west	lel ɣarb	للغرب
in the west	fel ɣarb	في الغرب
western (adj)	ɣarby	غربي
east	ʃarʾ (m)	شرق
to the east	lel ʃarʾ	للشرق
in the east	fel ʃarʾ	في الشرق
eastern (adj)	ʃarʾy	شرقي

77. Sea. Ocean

sea	baḥr (m)	بحر
ocean	moḥīṭ (m)	محيط
gulf (bay)	χalīg (m)	خليج
straits	maḍīq (m)	مضيق
land (solid ground)	barr (m)	برّ
continent (mainland)	qārra (f)	قارّة
island	gezīra (f)	جزيرة
peninsula	ʃebh gezeyra (f)	شبه جزيرة
archipelago	magmūʿet gozor (f)	مجموعة جزر
bay, cove	χalīg (m)	خليج
harbor	mināʾ (m)	ميناء
lagoon	lagūn (m)	لاجون
cape	raʾs (m)	رأس
atoll	gezīra morganiya estwaʾiya (f)	جزيزة مرجانية إستوائيّة
reef	ʃoʿāb (pl)	شعاب
coral	morgān (m)	مرجان

coral reef	ʃo'āb morganiya (pl)	شعاب مرجانية
deep (adj)	'amīq	عميق
depth (deep water)	'omq (m)	عمق
abyss	el 'omq el saḥīq (m)	العمق السحيق
trench (e.g., Mariana ~)	χondoq (m)	خندق
current (Ocean ~)	tayār (m)	تيّار
to surround (bathe)	ḥāṭ	حاط
shore	sāḥel (m)	ساحل
coast	sāḥel (m)	ساحل
flow (flood tide)	tayār (m)	تيّار
ebb (ebb tide)	gozor (m)	جزر
shoal	meyāh ḍaḥla (f)	مياه ضحلة
bottom (~ of the sea)	qā' (m)	قاع
wave	mouga (f)	موجة
crest (~ of a wave)	qemma (f)	قمّة
spume (sea foam)	zabad el baḥr (m)	زبد البحر
storm (sea storm)	'āṣefa (f)	عاصفة
hurricane	e'ṣār (m)	إعصار
tsunami	tsunāmy (m)	تسونامي
calm (dead ~)	hodū' (m)	هدوء
quiet, calm (adj)	hady	هادئ
pole	'oṭb (m)	قطب
polar (adj)	'oṭby	قطبي
latitude	'arḍ (m)	عرض
longitude	χaṭṭ ṭūl (m)	خطّ طول
parallel	motawāz (m)	متواز
equator	χaṭṭ el estewā' (m)	خطّ الإستواء
sky	samā' (f)	سماء
horizon	ofoq (m)	أفق
air	hawā' (m)	هواء
lighthouse	manāra (f)	منارة
to dive (vi)	ɣāṣ	غاص
to sink (ab. boat)	ɣere'	غرق
treasures	konūz (pl)	كنوز

78. Seas' and Oceans' names

Atlantic Ocean	el moḥeyṭ el aṭlanty (m)	المحيط الأطلنطي
Indian Ocean	el moḥeyṭ el hendy (m)	المحيط الهندي
Pacific Ocean	el moḥeyṭ el hādy (m)	المحيط الهادي
Arctic Ocean	el moḥeyṭ el motagammed el ʃamāly (m)	المحيط المتجمّد الشمالي

Black Sea	el bahr el aswad (m)	البحر الأسود
Red Sea	el bahr el ahmar (m)	البحر الأحمر
Yellow Sea	el bahr el asfar (m)	البحر الأصفر
White Sea	el bahr el abyaḍ (m)	البحر الأبيض
Caspian Sea	bahr qazwīn (m)	بحر قزوين
Dead Sea	el bahr el mayet (m)	البحر الميّت
Mediterranean Sea	el bahr el abyaḍ el motawasseṭ (m)	البحر الأبيض المتوسّط
Aegean Sea	bahr eygah (m)	بحر إيجة
Adriatic Sea	el bahr el adreyatīky (m)	البحر الأدرياتيكي
Arabian Sea	bahr el 'arab (m)	بحر العرب
Sea of Japan	bahr el yabān (m)	بحر اليابان
Bering Sea	bahr bering (m)	بحر بيرينغ
South China Sea	bahr el ṣeyn el ganūby (m)	بحر الصين الجنوبي
Coral Sea	bahr el morgān (m)	بحر المرجان
Tasman Sea	bahr tazman (m)	بحر تسمان
Caribbean Sea	el bahr el karība (m)	البحر الكاريبي
Barents Sea	bahr barents (m)	بحر بارنتس
Kara Sea	bahr kara (m)	بحر كارا
North Sea	bahr el ʃamāl (m)	بحر الشمال
Baltic Sea	bahr el baltīq (m)	بحر البلطيق
Norwegian Sea	bahr el nerwīg (m)	بحر النرويج

79. Mountains

mountain	gabal (m)	جبل
mountain range	selselet gebāl (f)	سلسلة جبال
mountain ridge	notū' el gabal (m)	نتوء الجبل
summit, top	qemma (f)	قمّة
peak	qemma (f)	قمّة
foot (~ of the mountain)	asfal (m)	أسفل
slope (mountainside)	monhadar (m)	منحدر
volcano	borkān (m)	بركان
active volcano	borkān naʃeṭ (m)	بركان نشط
dormant volcano	borkān χāmed (m)	بركان خامد
eruption	sawarān (m)	ثوّران
crater	fawhet el borkān (f)	فوهة البركان
magma	magma (f)	ماجما
lava	homam borkāniya (pl)	حمم بركانية
molten (~ lava)	monṣahera	منصهرة
canyon	wādy ḍaye' (m)	وادي ضيّق

gorge	mamarr ḍaye' (m)	ممرّ ضيّق
crevice	ʃa'' (m)	شقّ
abyss (chasm)	hāwya (f)	هاوية
pass, col	mamarr gabaly (m)	ممرّ جبلي
plateau	haḍaba (f)	هضبة
cliff	garf (m)	جرف
hill	tall (m)	تلّ
glacier	nahr galīdy (m)	نهر جليدي
waterfall	ʃallāl (m)	شلّال
geyser	nab' maya ḥāra (m)	نبع ميّة حارة
lake	boḥeyra (f)	بحيرة
plain	sahl (m)	سهل
landscape	manzar ṭabee'y (m)	منظر طبيعي
echo	ṣada (m)	صدى
alpinist	motasalleq el gebāl (m)	متسلّق الجبال
rock climber	motasalleq ṣoχūr (m)	متسلّق صخور
to conquer (in climbing)	taɣallab 'ala	تغلّب على
climb (an easy ~)	tasalloq (m)	تسلّق

80. Mountains names

The Alps	gebāl el alb (pl)	جبال الألب
Mont Blanc	mōn blōn (m)	مون بلون
The Pyrenees	gebāl el barānes (pl)	جبال البرانس
The Carpathians	gebāl el karbāt (pl)	جبال الكاربات
The Ural Mountains	gebāl el urāl (pl)	جبال الأورال
The Caucasus Mountains	gebāl el qoqāz (pl)	جبال القوقاز
Mount Elbrus	gabal elbrus (m)	جبل إلبروس
The Altai Mountains	gebāl altāy (pl)	جبال ألتاي
The Tian Shan	gebāl tian ʃan (pl)	جبال تيان شان
The Pamir Mountains	gebāl bamir (pl)	جبال بامير
The Himalayas	himalāya (pl)	هيمالايا
Mount Everest	gabal everest (m)	جبل افرست
The Andes	gebāl el andīz (pl)	جبال الأنديز
Mount Kilimanjaro	gabal kilimanʒaro (m)	جبل كليمنجارو

81. Rivers

river	nahr (m)	نهر
spring (natural source)	'eyn (m)	عين
riverbed (river channel)	magra el nahr (m)	مجرى النهر

basin (river valley)	ḥoḍe (m)	حوض
to flow into …	ṣabb fe …	صبَّ في...
tributary	rāfed (m)	رافد
bank (of river)	ḍaffa (f)	ضفّة
current (stream)	tayār (m)	تيّار
downstream (adv)	maʿ ettigāh magra el nahr	مع إتّجاه مجرى النهر
upstream (adv)	ḍed el tayār	ضد التيار
inundation	ɣamr (m)	غمر
flooding	fayaḍān (m)	فيضان
to overflow (vi)	fāḍ	فاض
to flood (vt)	ɣamar	غمر
shallow (shoal)	meyāh ḍaḥla (f)	مياه ضحلة
rapids	monḥadar el nahr (m)	منحدر النهر
dam	sadd (m)	سدَّ
canal	qanah (f)	قناة
reservoir (artificial lake)	χazzān māʾy (m)	خزّان مائي
sluice, lock	bawwāba qanṭara (f)	بوّابة قنطرة
water body (pond, etc.)	berka (f)	بركة
swamp (marshland)	mostanqaʿ (m)	مستنقع
bog, marsh	mostanqaʿ (m)	مستنقع
whirlpool	dawwāma (f)	دوّامة
stream (brook)	gadwal (m)	جدوَل
drinking (ab. water)	el ʃorb	الشرب
fresh (~ water)	ʿazb	عذب
ice	galīd (m)	جليد
to freeze over (ab. river, etc.)	etgammed	إتجمَّد

82. Rivers' names

Seine	el seyn (m)	السين
Loire	el lua:r (m)	اللوار
Thames	el teymz (m)	التيمز
Rhine	el rayn (m)	الراين
Danube	el danūb (m)	الدانوب
Volga	el volga (m)	الفولغا
Don	el done (m)	الدون
Lena	lena (m)	لينا
Yellow River	el nahr el aṣfar (m)	النهر الأصفر
Yangtze	el yangesty (m)	اليانغستي

Mekong	el mekong (m)	الميكونغ
Ganges	el ɣang (m)	الغانج
Nile River	el nīl (m)	النيل
Congo River	el kongo (m)	الكونغو
Okavango River	okavango (m)	أوكافانجو
Zambezi River	el zambizi (m)	الزمبيزي
Limpopo River	limbobo (m)	ليمبوبو
Mississippi River	el mississibbi (m)	الميسيسيبي

83. Forest

forest, wood	ɣāba (f)	غابة
forest (as adj)	ɣāba	غابة
thick forest	ɣāba kasīfa (f)	غابة كثيفة
grove	bostān (m)	بستان
forest clearing	ezālet el ɣābāt (f)	إزالة الغابات
thicket	agama (f)	أجمة
scrubland	arāḍy el ʃogayrāt (pl)	أراضي الشجيرات
footpath (troddenpath)	mamarr (m)	ممرّ
gully	wādy ḍaye' (m)	وادي ضيّق
tree	ʃagara (f)	شجرة
leaf	wara'a (f)	ورقة
leaves (foliage)	wara' (m)	ورق
fall of leaves	tasā'oṭ el awrā' (m)	تساقط الأوراق
to fall (ab. leaves)	saqaṭ	سقط
top (of the tree)	ra's (m)	رأس
branch	ɣoṣn (m)	غصن
bough	ɣoṣn ra'īsy (m)	غصن رئيسي
bud (on shrub, tree)	bor'om (m)	برعم
needle (of pine tree)	ʃawka (f)	شوكة
pine cone	kūz el ṣnowbar (m)	كوز الصنوبر
hollow (in a tree)	gofe (m)	جوف
nest	'eʃ (m)	عشّ
burrow (animal hole)	goḥr (m)	جحر
trunk	gez' (m)	جذع
root	gezr (m)	جذر
bark	leḥā' (m)	لحاء
moss	ṭaḥlab (m)	طحلب
to uproot (remove trees or tree stumps)	eqtala'	إقتلع

to chop down	'aṭṭa'	قطّع
to deforest (vt)	azāl el ɣabāt	أزال الغابات
tree stump	gez' el ʃagara (m)	جذع الشجرة
campfire	nār moχayem (m)	نار مخيّم
forest fire	ḥarī' ɣāba (m)	حريق غابة
to extinguish (vt)	ṭaffa	طفّى
forest ranger	ḥāres el ɣāba (m)	حارس الغابة
protection	ḥemāya (f)	حماية
to protect (~ nature)	ḥama	حمى
poacher	sāre' el ṣeyd (m)	سارق الصيد
steel trap	maṣyada (f)	مصيدة
to gather, to pick (vt)	gamma'	جمّع
to lose one's way	tāh	تاه

84. Natural resources

natural resources	sarawāt ṭabi'iya (pl)	ثروات طبيعيّة
minerals	ma'āden (pl)	معادن
deposits	rawāseb (pl)	رواسب
field (e.g., oilfield)	ḥaql (m)	حقل
to mine (extract)	estaχrag	إستخرج
mining (extraction)	esteχrāg (m)	إستخراج
ore	χām (m)	خام
mine (e.g., for coal)	mangam (m)	منجم
shaft (mine ~)	mangam (m)	منجم
miner	'āmel mangam (m)	عامل منجم
gas (natural ~)	ɣāz (m)	غاز
gas pipeline	χaṭṭ anabīb ɣāz (m)	خطّ أنابيب غاز
oil (petroleum)	nafṭ (m)	نفط
oil pipeline	anabīb el nafṭ (pl)	أنابيب النفط
oil well	bīr el nafṭ (m)	بير النفط
derrick (tower)	ḥaffāra (f)	حفّارة
tanker	nāqelet betrūl (f)	ناقلة بترول
sand	raml (m)	رمل
limestone	ḥagar el kals (m)	حجر الكلس
gravel	ḥaṣa (m)	حصى
peat	χaθ faḥm nabāty (m)	خث فحم نباتي
clay	ṭīn (m)	طين
coal	faḥm (m)	فحم
iron (ore)	ḥadīd (m)	حديد
gold	dahab (m)	ذهب
silver	faḍḍa (f)	فضّة

nickel	nikel (m)	نيكل
copper	neḥās (m)	نحاس
zinc	zink (m)	زنك
manganese	manganīz (m)	منجنيز
mercury	ze'baq (m)	زئبق
lead	roṣāṣ (m)	رصاص
mineral	ma'dan (m)	معدن
crystal	kristāl (m)	كريستال
marble	roχām (m)	رخام
uranium	yuranuim (m)	يورانيوم

85. Weather

weather	ṭa's (m)	طقس
weather forecast	naʃra gawiya (f)	نشرة جويّة
temperature	ḥarāra (f)	حرارة
thermometer	termometr (m)	ترمومتر
barometer	barometr (m)	بارومتر
humid (adj)	roṭob	رطب
humidity	roṭūba (f)	رطوبة
heat (extreme ~)	ḥarāra (f)	حرارة
hot (torrid)	ḥarr	حارّ
it's hot	el gaww ḥarr	الجّو حرّ
it's warm	el gaww dafa	الجوّ دفا
warm (moderately hot)	dāfe'	دافئ
it's cold	el gaww bāred	الجوّ بارد
cold (adj)	bāred	بارد
sun	ʃams (f)	شمس
to shine (vi)	nawwar	نوّر
sunny (day)	moʃmes	مشمس
to come up (vi)	ʃara'	شرق
to set (vi)	ɣarab	غرب
cloud	saḥāba (f)	سحابة
cloudy (adj)	meɣayem	مغيّم
rain cloud	saḥābet maṭar (f)	سحابة مطر
somber (gloomy)	meɣayem	مغيّم
rain	maṭar (m)	مطر
it's raining	el donia betmaṭṭar	الدنيا بتمطّر
rainy (~ day, weather)	momṭer	ممطر
to drizzle (vi)	maṭṭaret razāz	مطّرت رذاذ
pouring rain	maṭar monhamer (f)	مطر منهمر
downpour	maṭar ɣazīr (m)	مطر غزير

heavy (e.g., ~ rain)	ʃedīd	شديد
puddle	berka (f)	بركة
to get wet (in rain)	ettbal	إتّبل
fog (mist)	ʃabbūra (f)	شبّورة
foggy	fih ʃabbūra	فيه شبّورة
snow	talg (m)	ثلج
it's snowing	fih talg	فيه ثلج

86. Severe weather. Natural disasters

thunderstorm	ʿāṣefa raʿdiya (f)	عاصفة رعدية
lightning (~ strike)	barʾ (m)	برق
to flash (vi)	baraq	برق
thunder	raʿd (m)	رعد
to thunder (vi)	dawa	دوّى
it's thundering	el samāʾ dawat raʿd (f)	السماء دوّت رعد
hail	maṭar bard (m)	مطر برد
it's hailing	maṭṭaret bard	مطّرت برد
to flood (vt)	ɣamar	غمر
flood, inundation	fayaḍān (m)	فيضان
earthquake	zelzāl (m)	زلزال
tremor, quake	hazza arḍiya (f)	هزّة أرضية
epicenter	markaz el zelzāl (m)	مركز الزلزال
eruption	sawarān (m)	ثوّران
lava	ḥomam borkāniya (pl)	حمم بركانية
twister, tornado	eʿṣār (m)	إعصار
typhoon	tyfūn (m)	طوفان
hurricane	eʿṣār (m)	إعصار
storm	ʿāṣefa (f)	عاصفة
tsunami	tsunāmy (m)	تسونامي
cyclone	eʿṣār (m)	إعصار
bad weather	ṭaʾs sayeʾ (m)	طقس سئ
fire (accident)	ḥarīʾ (m)	حريق
disaster	karsa (f)	كارثة
meteorite	nayzek (m)	نيّزك
avalanche	enheyār talgy (m)	إنهيار ثلجي
snowslide	enheyār talgy (m)	إنهيار ثلجي
blizzard	ʿāṣefa talgiya (f)	عاصفة ثلجيّة
snowstorm	ʿāṣefa talgiya (f)	عاصفة ثلجيّة

FAUNA

87. Mammals. Predators

predator	moftares (m)	مفترس
tiger	nemr (m)	نمر
lion	asad (m)	أسد
wolf	ze'b (m)	ذئب
fox	ta'lab (m)	ثعلب
jaguar	nemr amrīky (m)	نمر أمريكي
leopard	fahd (m)	فهد
cheetah	fahd ṣayād (m)	فهد صيّاد
black panther	nemr aswad (m)	نمر أسوّد
puma	asad el gebāl (m)	أسد الجبال
snow leopard	nemr el tolūg (m)	نمر الثلوج
lynx	waʃaq (m)	وشق
coyote	qayūṭ (m)	قيوط
jackal	ebn 'āwy (m)	ابن آوى
hyena	ḍeb' (m)	ضبع

88. Wild animals

animal	ḥayawān (m)	حيوان
beast (animal)	waḥʃ (m)	وحش
squirrel	sengāb (m)	سنجاب
hedgehog	qonfoz (m)	قنفذ
hare	arnab barry (m)	أرنب برّي
rabbit	arnab (m)	أرنب
badger	ɣarīr (m)	غرير
raccoon	rakūn (m)	راكون
hamster	hamster (m)	هامستر
marmot	marmoṭ (m)	مرموط
mole	χold (m)	خلد
mouse	fār (m)	فأر
rat	gerz (m)	جرذ
bat	χoffāʃ (m)	خفّاش
ermine	qāqem (m)	قاقِم
sable	sammūr (m)	سمّور

marten	fara'īāt (m)	فرائيات
weasel	ebn 'ers (m)	ابن عرس
mink	mink (m)	منك
beaver	qondos (m)	قندس
otter	ta'lab maya (m)	ثعلب الميّة
horse	ḥoṣān (m)	حصان
moose	eyl el mūz (m)	أيّل الموظ
deer	ayl (m)	أيل
camel	gamal (m)	جمل
bison	bison (m)	بيسون
aurochs	byson orobby (m)	بيسون أوروبي
buffalo	gamūs (m)	جاموس
zebra	ḥomār waḥʃy (m)	حمار وحشي
antelope	ẓaby (m)	ظبي
roe deer	yaḥmūr orobby (m)	يحمورأوروبيّ
fallow deer	eyl asmar orobby (m)	أيّل أسمر أوروبي
chamois	ʃamwah (f)	شاموّاه
wild boar	χenzīr barry (m)	خنزير برّي
whale	ḥūt (m)	حوت
seal	foqma (f)	فقمة
walrus	el kab' (m)	الكبع
fur seal	foqmet el farā' (f)	فقمة الفراء
dolphin	dolfīn (m)	دولفين
bear	dobb (m)	دبّ
polar bear	dobb 'oṭṭby (m)	دبّ قطبي
panda	banda (m)	باندا
monkey	'erd (m)	قرد
chimpanzee	ʃimbanzy (m)	شيمبانزي
orangutan	orangutan (m)	أورنغوتان
gorilla	ɣorella (f)	غوريلا
macaque	'erd el makāk (m)	قرد المكاك
gibbon	gibbon (m)	جيبون
elephant	fīl (m)	فيل
rhinoceros	χartīt (m)	خرتيت
giraffe	zarāfa (f)	زرافة
hippopotamus	faras el nahr (m)	فرس النهر
kangaroo	kangarū (m)	كانجّارو
koala (bear)	el koala (m)	الكوالا
mongoose	nems (m)	نمس
chinchilla	ʃenʃīla (f)	شنشيلة
skunk	ẓerbān (m)	ظربان
porcupine	nīṣ (m)	نيص

89. Domestic animals

cat	ʼoṭṭa (f)	قطّة
tomcat	ʼoṭṭ (m)	قطّ
dog	kalb (m)	كلب
horse	ḥoṣān (m)	حصان
stallion (male horse)	χeyl faḥl (m)	خيل فحل
mare	faras (f)	فرس
cow	baʼara (f)	بقرة
bull	sore (m)	ثور
ox	sore (m)	ثور
sheep (ewe)	χarūf (f)	خروف
ram	kebʃ (m)	كبش
goat	meʿza (f)	معزة
billy goat, he-goat	māʿez zakar (m)	ماعز ذكر
donkey	ḥomār (m)	حمار
mule	baɣl (m)	بغل
pig, hog	χenzīr (m)	خنزير
piglet	χannūṣ (m)	خنّوص
rabbit	arnab (m)	أرنب
hen (chicken)	farχa (f)	فرخة
rooster	dīk (m)	ديك
duck	baṭṭa (f)	بطّة
drake	dakar el baṭṭ (m)	ذكر البط
goose	wezza (f)	وزّة
tom turkey, gobbler	dīk rūmy (m)	ديك رومي
turkey (hen)	dīk rūmy (m)	ديك رومي
domestic animals	ḥayawānāt dawāgen (pl)	حيوانات دواجن
tame (e.g., ~ hamster)	alīf	أليف
to tame (vt)	rawweḍ	روّض
to breed (vt)	rabba	ربّى
farm	mazraʿa (f)	مزرعة
poultry	dawāgen (pl)	دواجن
cattle	māʃeya (f)	ماشية
herd (cattle)	qaṭeeʿ (m)	قطيع
stable	esṭabl χeyl (m)	إسطبل خيل
pigpen	ḥazīret χanazīr (f)	حظيرة الخنازير
cowshed	zerībet el baʼar (f)	زريبة البقر
rabbit hutch	qan el arāneb (m)	قن الأرانب
hen house	qan el ferāχ (m)	قن الفراخ

90. Birds

bird	ṭā'er (m)	طائر
pigeon	ḥamāma (f)	حمامة
sparrow	'aṣfūr dawri (m)	عصفور دوري
tit (great tit)	qarqaf (m)	قرقف
magpie	'a''a' (m)	عقعق
raven	ɣorāb aswad (m)	غراب أسود
crow	ɣorāb (m)	غراب
jackdaw	zāɣ zar'y (m)	زاغ زرعي
rook	ɣorāb el qeyẓ (m)	غراب القيظ
duck	baṭṭa (f)	بطّة
goose	wezza (f)	وزّة
pheasant	tadarrog (m)	تدرج
eagle	'eqāb (m)	عقاب
hawk	el bāz (m)	الباز
falcon	ṣa'r (m)	صقر
vulture	nesr (m)	نسر
condor (Andean ~)	kondor (m)	كندور
swan	el temm (m)	التمّ
crane	karkiya (m)	كركية
stork	loqloq (m)	لقلق
parrot	babaɣā' (m)	ببغاء
hummingbird	ṭannān (m)	طنّان
peacock	ṭawūs (m)	طاووس
ostrich	na'āma (f)	نعامة
heron	belʃone (m)	بلشون
flamingo	flamingo (m)	فلامينجو
pelican	bag'a (f)	بجعة
nightingale	'andalīb (m)	عندليب
swallow	el sonūnū (m)	السنونو
thrush	somnet el ḥoqūl (m)	سمنة الحقول
song thrush	somna moɣarreda (m)	سمنة مغرّدة
blackbird	ʃaḥrūr aswad (m)	شحرور أسود
swift	semmāma (m)	سمّامة
lark	qabra (f)	قبرة
quail	semmān (m)	سمّان
woodpecker	na'ār el χaʃab (m)	نقار الخشب
cuckoo	weqwāq (m)	وقواق
owl	būma (f)	بومة
eagle owl	būm orāsy (m)	بوم أوراسي

wood grouse	dīk el χalang (m)	ديك الخلنج
black grouse	ţyhūg aswad (m)	طيهوج أسود
partridge	el ḥagal (m)	الحجل
starling	zerzūr (m)	زرزور
canary	kanāry (m)	كناري
hazel grouse	ţyhūg el bondo' (m)	طيهوج البندق
chaffinch	ʃarʃūr (m)	شرشور
bullfinch	deɣnāʃ (m)	دغناش
seagull	nawras (m)	نورس
albatross	el qoṭros (m)	القطرس
penguin	beṭrīq (m)	بطريق

91. Fish. Marine animals

bream	abramīs (m)	أبراميس
carp	ʃabbūṭ (m)	شبّوط
perch	farχ (m)	فرخ
catfish	'armūṭ (m)	قرموط
pike	karāky (m)	كراكي
salmon	salamon (m)	سلمون
sturgeon	ḥafʃ (m)	حفش
herring	renga (f)	رنجة
Atlantic salmon	salamon aṭlasy (m)	سلمون أطلسي
mackerel	makerel (m)	ماكريل
flatfish	samak mefalṭah (f)	سمك مفلطح
zander, pike perch	samak sandar (m)	سمك سندر
cod	el qadd (m)	القد
tuna	tuna (f)	تونة
trout	salamon mera''aṭ (m)	سلمون مرقّط
eel	ḥankalīs (m)	حنكليس
electric ray	ra'ād (m)	رعاد
moray eel	moraya (f)	موراية
piranha	bīrana (f)	بيرانا
shark	'erʃ (m)	قرش
dolphin	dolfīn (m)	دولفين
whale	ḥūt (m)	حوت
crab	kaboria (m)	كابوريا
jellyfish	'andīl el baḥr (m)	قنديل البحر
octopus	aχṭabūṭ (m)	أخطبوط
starfish	negmet el baḥr (f)	نجمة البحر
sea urchin	qonfoz el baḥr (m)	قنفذ البحر

seahorse	ḥoṣān el baḥr (m)	حصان البحر
oyster	maḥār (m)	محار
shrimp	gammbary (m)	جمّبري
lobster	estakoza (f)	استكوزا
spiny lobster	estakoza (m)	استاكوزا

92. Amphibians. Reptiles

snake	te'bān (m)	ثعبان
venomous (snake)	sām	سام
viper	af'a (f)	أفعى
cobra	kobra (m)	كوبرا
python	te'bān byton (m)	ثعبان بايثون
boa	bawā' el 'aṣera (f)	بواء العاصرة
grass snake	te'bān el 'oʃb (m)	ثعبان العشب
rattle snake	af'a megalgela (f)	أفعى مجلجلة
anaconda	anakonda (f)	أناكوندا
lizard	seḥliya (f)	سحليّة
iguana	eɣwana (f)	إغوانة
monitor lizard	warl (m)	ورل
salamander	salamander (m)	سلمندر
chameleon	ḥerbāya (f)	حرباية
scorpion	'a'rab (m)	عقرب
turtle	solḥefah (f)	سلحفاة
frog	ḍeffḍa' (m)	ضفدع
toad	ḍeffḍa' el ṭeyn (m)	ضفدع الطين
crocodile	temsāḥ (m)	تمساح

93. Insects

insect, bug	ḥaʃara (f)	حشرة
butterfly	farāʃa (f)	فراشة
ant	namla (f)	نملة
fly	debbāna (f)	دبّانة
mosquito	namūsa (f)	ناموسة
beetle	χonfesa (f)	خنفسة
wasp	dabbūr (m)	دبّور
bee	naḥla (f)	نحلة
bumblebee	naḥla ṭannāna (f)	نحلة طنّانة
gadfly (botfly)	na'ra (f)	نعرة
spider	'ankabūt (m)	عنكبوت
spiderweb	nasīg 'ankabūt (m)	نسيج عنكبوت

dragonfly	ya'sūb (m)	يعسوب
grasshopper	garād (m)	جراد
moth (night butterfly)	'etta (f)	عثّة
cockroach	ṣarṣūr (m)	صرصور
tick	qarāda (f)	قرادة
flea	barɣūt (m)	برغوث
midge	ba'ūḍa (f)	بعوضة
locust	garād (m)	جراد
snail	ḥalazōn (m)	حلزون
cricket	ṣarṣūr el ḥaql (m)	صرصور الحقل
lightning bug	yarā'a (f)	يراعة
ladybug	χonfesa mena'ṭṭa (f)	خنفسة منقّطة
cockchafer	χonfesa motlefa lel nabāt (f)	خنفسة متّلفة للنبات
leech	'alaqa (f)	علقة
caterpillar	yasrū' (m)	يسروع
earthworm	dūda (f)	دودة
larva	yaraqa (f)	يرقة

FLORA

94. Trees

tree	ʃagara (f)	شجرة
deciduous (adj)	nafḍiya	نفضيّة
coniferous (adj)	ṣonoberiya	صنوبرية
evergreen (adj)	dā'emet el χoḍra	دائمة الخضرة
apple tree	ʃagaret toffāḥ (f)	شجرة تفّاح
pear tree	ʃagaret komettra (f)	شجرة كمثّرى
cherry tree	ʃagaret karaz (f)	شجرة كرز
plum tree	ʃagaret bar'ū' (f)	شجرة برقوق
birch	batola (f)	بتولا
oak	ballūṭ (f)	بلّوط
linden tree	zayzafūn (f)	زيزفون
aspen	ḥūr rāgef	حور راجف
maple	qayqab (f)	قيقب
spruce	rateng (f)	راتينج
pine	ṣonober (f)	صنوبر
larch	arziya (f)	أرزية
fir tree	tanūb (f)	تنوب
cedar	el orz (f)	الأرز
poplar	ḥūr (f)	حور
rowan	ɣobayrā' (f)	غبيراء
willow	ṣefsāf (f)	صفصاف
alder	gār el mā' (m)	جار الماء
beech	el zān (f)	الزان
elm	derdar (f)	دردار
ash (tree)	marān (f)	مران
chestnut	kastanā' (f)	كستناء
magnolia	maɣnolia (f)	ماغنوليا
palm tree	naχla (f)	نخلة
cypress	el soro (f)	السرو
mangrove	mangrūf (f)	مانجروف
baobab	baobab (f)	باوباب
eucalyptus	eukalyptus (f)	أوكالبتوس
sequoia	sequoia (f)	سيكويا

95. Shrubs

bush	ʃogeyra (f)	شجيرة
shrub	ʃogayrāt (pl)	شجيرات
grapevine	karma (f)	كرمة
vineyard	karam (m)	كرم
raspberry bush	zarʿet tūt el ʿalīʾ el aḥmar (f)	زرعة توت العليق الأحمر
redcurrant bush	keʃmeʃ aḥmar (m)	كشمش أحمر
gooseberry bush	ʿenab el saʿlab (m)	عنب الثعلب
acacia	aqaqia (f)	أقاقيا
barberry	berbarīs (m)	برباريس
jasmine	yasmīn (m)	ياسمين
juniper	ʿarʿar (m)	عرعر
rosebush	ʃogeyret ward (f)	شجيرة ورد
dog rose	ward el seyāg (pl)	ورد السياج

96. Fruits. Berries

fruit	tamra (f)	تمرة
fruits	tamr (m)	تمر
apple	toffāḥa (f)	تفّاحة
pear	komettra (f)	كمّثرى
plum	barʾūʾ (m)	برقوق
strawberry (garden ~)	farawla (f)	فراولة
cherry	karaz (m)	كرز
grape	ʿenab (m)	عنب
raspberry	tūt el ʿalīʾ el aḥmar (m)	توت العليق الأحمر
blackcurrant	keʃmeʃ aswad (m)	كشمش أسود
redcurrant	keʃmeʃ aḥmar (m)	كشمش أحمر
gooseberry	ʿenab el saʿlab (m)	عنب الثعلب
cranberry	ʿenabiya ḥāda el χebāʾ (m)	عنبية حادة الخباء
orange	bortoqāl (m)	برتقال
mandarin	yosfy (m)	يوسفي
pineapple	ananās (m)	أناناس
banana	moze (m)	موز
date	tamr (m)	تمر
lemon	lymūn (m)	ليمون
apricot	meʃmeʃ (f)	مشمش
peach	χawχa (f)	خوخة
kiwi	kiwi (m)	كيوي
grapefruit	grabe frūt (m)	جريب فروت

berry	tūt (m)	توت
berries	tūt (pl)	توت
cowberry	ʻenab el sore (m)	عنب الثور
wild strawberry	farawla barriya (f)	فراولة برّيّة
bilberry	ʻenab al aḥrāg (m)	عنب الأحراج

97. Flowers. Plants

flower	zahra (f)	زهرة
bouquet (of flowers)	bokeyh (f)	بوكيه
rose (flower)	warda (f)	وردة
tulip	tolīb (f)	توليب
carnation	ʼoronfol (m)	قرنفل
gladiolus	el dalbūs (f)	الدّلَبُوث
cornflower	qanṭeryūn ʻanbary (m)	قنطريون عنبري
harebell	garīs mostadīr el awrāʼ (m)	جريس مستدير الأوراق
dandelion	handabāʼ (f)	هندباء
camomile	kamomile (f)	كاموميل
aloe	el alowa (m)	الألوّة
cactus	ṣabbār (m)	صبّار
rubber plant, ficus	faykas (m)	فيّكس
lily	zanbaq (f)	زنبق
geranium	ɣarnūqy (f)	غرنوقي
hyacinth	el lavender (f)	اللافندر
mimosa	mimoza (f)	ميموزا
narcissus	nerges (f)	نرجس
nasturtium	abo χangar (f)	أبو خنجر
orchid	orkid (f)	أوركيد
peony	fawnia (f)	فاوانيا
violet	el banafseg (f)	البنفسج
pansy	bansy (f)	بانسي
forget-me-not	ʼāzān el faʼr (pl)	آذان الفأر
daisy	aqwaḥān (f)	أقحوان
poppy	el χoʃχāʃ (f)	الخشخاش
hemp	qanb (m)	قنب
mint	neʻnāʻ (m)	نعناع
lily of the valley	zanbaq el wādy (f)	زنبق الوادي
snowdrop	zahrat el laban (f)	زهرة اللبن
nettle	ʼarrāṣ (m)	قرّاص
sorrel	ḥammāḍ bostāny (m)	حمّاض بستاني

water lily	niloferiya (f)	نيلوفرية
fern	sarχas (m)	سرخس
lichen	aʃna (f)	أشنة
greenhouse (tropical ~)	ṣoba (f)	صوبة
lawn	ʻoʃb aχḍar (m)	عشب أخضر
flowerbed	geneynet zohūr (f)	جنينة زهور
plant	nabāt (m)	نبات
grass	ʻoʃb (m)	عشب
blade of grass	ʻoʃba (f)	عشبة
leaf	wara'a (f)	ورقة
petal	wara'et el zahra (f)	ورقة الزهرة
stem	sāq (f)	ساق
tuber	darna (f)	درنة
young plant (shoot)	nabta saɣīra (f)	نبتة صغيرة
thorn	ʃawka (f)	شوكة
to blossom (vi)	fattaḥet	فتّحت
to fade, to wither	debel	ذبل
smell (odor)	rīḥa (f)	ريحة
to cut (flowers)	'aṭaʻ	قطع
to pick (a flower)	'aṭaf	قطف

98. Cereals, grains

grain	ḥobūb (pl)	حبوب
cereal crops	maḥaṣīl el ḥubūb (pl)	محاصيل الحبوب
ear (of barley, etc.)	sonbola (f)	سنبلة
wheat	'amḥ (m)	قمح
rye	ʃelm mazrūʻ (m)	شيلم مزروع
oats	ʃofān (m)	شوفان
millet	el deχn (m)	الدُخن
barley	ʃeʻīr (m)	شعير
corn	dora (f)	ذرة
rice	rozz (m)	رز
buckwheat	ḥanṭa soda' (f)	حنطة سوداء
pea plant	besella (f)	بسلّة
kidney bean	faṣolya (f)	فاصوليا
soy	fūl el ṣoya (m)	فول الصويا
lentil	ʻads (m)	عدس
beans (pulse crops)	fūl (m)	فول

COUNTRIES OF THE WORLD

99. Countries. Part 1

Afghanistan	afɣanistan (f)	أفغانستان
Albania	albānia (f)	ألبانيا
Argentina	arʒantīn (f)	الأرجنتين
Armenia	armīnia (f)	أرمينيا
Australia	ostorālya (f)	أستراليا
Austria	el nemsa (f)	النمسا
Azerbaijan	azrabiʒān (m)	أذربيجان
The Bahamas	gozor el bahāmas (pl)	جزر البهاماس
Bangladesh	bangladeʃ (f)	بنجلاديش
Belarus	belarūsia (f)	بيلاروسيا
Belgium	balʒīka (f)	بلجيكا
Bolivia	bolivia (f)	بوليفيا
Bosnia and Herzegovina	el bosna wel harsek (f)	البوسنة والهرسك
Brazil	el barazīl (f)	البرازيل
Bulgaria	bolɣāria (f)	بلغاريا
Cambodia	kambodya (f)	كمبوديا
Canada	kanada (f)	كندا
Chile	tʃīly (f)	تشيلي
China	el ṣīn (f)	الصين
Colombia	kolombia (f)	كولومبيا
Croatia	kroātya (f)	كرواتيا
Cuba	kūba (f)	كوبا
Cyprus	'obroṣ (f)	قبرص
Czech Republic	gomhoriya el tʃīk (f)	جمهورية التشيك
Denmark	el denmark (f)	الدنمارك
Dominican Republic	gomhoriya el dominikan (f)	جمهوريّة الدومينيكان
Ecuador	el equador (f)	الإكوادور
Egypt	maṣr (f)	مصر
England	engeltera (f)	إنجلّترا
Estonia	estūnia (f)	إستونيا
Finland	finlanda (f)	فنلّندا
France	faransa (f)	فرنسا
French Polynesia	bolenezia el faransiya (f)	بولينزيا الفرنسيّة
Georgia	ʒorʒia (f)	جورجيا
Germany	almānya (f)	ألمانيا
Ghana	ɣana (f)	غانا
Great Britain	briṭaniya el 'ozma (f)	بريطانيا العظمى
Greece	el yunān (f)	اليونان

Haiti	haīti (f)	هايتي
Hungary	el magar (f)	المجر

100. Countries. Part 2

Iceland	'āyslanda (f)	آيسلندا
India	el hend (f)	الهند
Indonesia	indonisya (f)	إندونيسيا
Iran	iran (f)	إيران
Iraq	el 'erāq (m)	العراق
Ireland	irelanda (f)	أيرلندا
Israel	isra'īl (f)	إسرائيل
Italy	eṭālia (f)	إيطاليا
Jamaica	ʒamayka (f)	جامايكا
Japan	el yabān (f)	اليابان
Jordan	el ordon (m)	الأردن
Kazakhstan	kazaχistān (f)	كازاخستّان
Kenya	kenya (f)	كينيا
Kirghizia	qirɣizestān (f)	قيرغيزستان
Kuwait	el kuweyt (f)	الكويت
Laos	laos (f)	لاوس
Latvia	latvia (f)	لاتفيا
Lebanon	lebnān (f)	لبنان
Libya	libya (f)	ليبيا
Liechtenstein	liʃtenʃtayn (m)	ليشتنشتاين
Lithuania	litwānia (f)	ليتوانيا
Luxembourg	luksemburg (f)	لوكسمبورج
Macedonia (Republic of ~)	maqdūnia (f)	مقدونيا
Madagascar	madaɣaʃkar (f)	مدغشقر
Malaysia	malīzya (f)	ماليزيا
Malta	malṭa (f)	مالطا
Mexico	el maksīk (f)	المكسيك
Moldova, Moldavia	moldāvia (f)	مولدافيا
Monaco	monako (f)	موناكو
Mongolia	manɣūlia (f)	منغوليا
Montenegro	el gabal el aswad (m)	الجبل الأسوّد
Morocco	el maɣreb (m)	المغرب
Myanmar	myanmar (f)	ميانمار
Namibia	namibia (f)	ناميبيا
Nepal	nebāl (f)	نيبال
Netherlands	holanda (f)	هولندا
New Zealand	nyu zelanda (f)	نيوزيلنّدا
North Korea	korea el ʃamāliya (f)	كوريا الشماليّة
Norway	el nerwīg (f)	النرويج

101. Countries. Part 3

Pakistan	bakistān (f)	باكستان
Palestine	felesṭīn (f)	فلسطين
Panama	banama (f)	بنما
Paraguay	baraguay (f)	باراجواي
Peru	beru (f)	بيرو
Poland	bolanda (f)	بولّندا
Portugal	el bortoɣāl (f)	البرتغال
Romania	romānia (f)	رومانيا
Russia	rūsya (f)	روسيا
Saudi Arabia	el so'odiya (f)	السعوديّة
Scotland	oskotlanda (f)	اسكتّلندا
Senegal	el senɣāl (f)	السنغال
Serbia	ṣerbia (f)	صربيا
Slovakia	slovākia (f)	سلوفاكيا
Slovenia	slovenia (f)	سلوفينيا
South Africa	afreqia el ganūbiya (f)	أفريقيا الجنوبيّة
South Korea	korea el ganūbiya (f)	كوريا الجنوبيّة
Spain	asbānya (f)	إسبانيا
Suriname	surinam (f)	سورينام
Sweden	el sweyd (f)	السويد
Switzerland	swesra (f)	سويسرا
Syria	soria (f)	سوريا
Taiwan	taywān (f)	تايوان
Tajikistan	ṭaʒīkistan (f)	طاجيكستان
Tanzania	tanznia (f)	تنزانيا
Tasmania	tasmania (f)	تاسمانيا
Thailand	tayland (f)	تايلاند
Tunisia	tunis (f)	تونس
Turkey	turkia (f)	تركيا
Turkmenistan	turkmānistān (f)	تركمانستان
Ukraine	okrānia (f)	أوكرانيا
United Arab Emirates	el emārāt el 'arabiya el mottaḥeda (pl)	الإمارات العربية المتّحدة
United States of America	el welayāt el mottaḥda el amrīkiya (pl)	الولايات المتّحدة الأمريكيّة
Uruguay	uruguay (f)	أوروجواي
Uzbekistan	uzbakistān (f)	أوزبكستان
Vatican	el vatikān (m)	الفاتيكان
Venezuela	venzweyla (f)	فنزويلا
Vietnam	vietnām (f)	فيتنام
Zanzibar	zanʒibār (f)	زنجبار

www.ingramcontent.com/pod-product-compliance
Lightning Source LLC
Chambersburg PA
CBHW070815050426
42452CB00011B/2059
* 9 7 8 1 7 8 7 1 6 7 0 6 3 *